D0255433

Spotlight on Leadership and School Change

Edited by Nancy Walser
and Caroline Chauncey

HARVARD EDUCATION PRESS
CAMBRIDGE, MASSACHUSETTS

Library of Congress Control Number 2007928176

Paperback ISBN 978-1-891792-47-2
Library Edition ISBN 978-1-891792-48-9

Published by Harvard Education Press,
an imprint of the Harvard Education Publishing Group

Harvard Education Press
8 Story Street
Cambridge, MA 02138

Cover Design: Perry Lubin

The typefaces used in this book are Humanst 777 for text and Kuenstler 480 for display.

Contents

Foreword

by Michael Fullan

I n *Spotlight on Leadership and School Change*, the editors of the *Harvard Education Letter* focus a powerful beam on one of the key issues in lasting school reform: the role of leadership. The five parts of this book address the different roles and spheres in which school leaders can bring about, sustain, and build on efforts to improve education for every child.

In our own work on education reform, my colleagues and I have become increasingly focused on what we call the "trilevel solution"—what has to happen at the school/community, district, and government levels in order to get large-scale success (see American Educational Research Association, 2007; Fullan, 2007). All of these efforts present significant leadership challenges.

We can identify the key things we know. On the obvious side (yet still difficult to implement on a wide scale) we know that:

1. Teachers who are strong on content and pedagogical knowledge and who care deeply (have moral purpose) about learning and students are more effective.

2. Teachers who use internal (assessment for learning) and external (assessment of learning) data on an ongoing basis

for both improving learning and marking progress are more effective.

3. Teachers who learn from others (again, on an ongoing basis) inside and outside the school are more effective.
4. Teachers who are led by principals and other school leaders who foster the first three qualities are more effective.
5. Teachers in districts that focus on creating districtwide cultures that develop and cultivate the previous four elements are more effective.
6. Teachers in state systems that integrate accountability and capacity-building while establishing partnerships across the three levels (school/community, district, and state) are more effective.

The qualities of teachers and the conditions under which they work are powerfully related to whether we will have enough teachers on any scale to invest and sustain the energy and actions necessary for continuous improvement. Susan Moore Johnson's (2004) *Finders and Keepers* makes it painfully clear that high-quality teachers will come and stay (all the while getting better) only under supportive and—let's be clear—demanding conditions. By this I mean conditions and cultures that have very high expectations for adults and students and pursue them relentlessly through a combination of support and accountability.

Chris Day and his colleagues (2007) in England have even more definitively demonstrated that teachers matter. Teachers in their sample who sustained a commitment over time did so because of a combination of leadership, collaborative colleagues, and personal support from family and friends (something less well studied in North America). Teachers with a declining commitment did so because of "workload," "pupil behavior," and "poor or unsupportive leadership"— the very things that effective organizations address.

Despite this growing clarity of evidence, we are not good at implementing strategies in a deep, comprehensive fashion. Most of the obvious solutions—focus on standards, provide mentoring, establish professional learning communities—turn out to be superficial. This is not because they are not on the right track, but because they fail to realize that other, more fundamental conditions need to be at the core of any effort. And these core conditions, which I will spell out briefly, are difficult to change. Let me put it dramatically via Peter Cole's (2004) wry article, "Professional Development: A Good Way to Avoid Change": Professional development is workshops, and no matter how relevant they are, it is not the same as learning every day. It *feels* like progress but in reality does not have an impact.

Richard Elmore (2004), a leading contributor to this volume, nailed the problem when he observed that

> improvement is . . . a function of *learning to do the right things* in the setting where you work. (p. 73, italics in original)

Alas,

> the problem [is that] there is almost no opportunity for teachers to engage in continuous and substantial learning about their practice in the settings in which they actually work, observing and being observed by their colleagues in their classrooms and [in] classrooms of other teachers in other schools confronting similar problems. (p. 127)

These are profound conclusions. Only a radical change in the working conditions of schools—and indeed in the entire culture of the teaching profession—will produce continuous learning on a large scale.

In *Breakthrough* (Fullan, Hill, & Crévola, 2006), we set out what it will take for this to happen. We argued that three Ps need to be put in place: precision, personalization, and personal learning. Precision and personalization are about meeting the unique needs of every student on a timely and precise basis. Professional learning (note that we did *not* say professional development) consists of every teacher learning every day, individually and collectively. The entire system must be organized to make this happen.

It is not just a matter of providing new opportunities and supportive conditions. There are deep structural and cultural barriers to be overcome. In *Breakthrough* we reported that several major, high-profile, well-funded districtwide reform efforts failed to get inside the classroom on any scale, and that this "deprivatization" of teaching still represents a huge cultural and structural barrier. Until it becomes normal for all teachers to observe one anothers' teaching facilitated by teacher leaders and other experts, we will not have the conditions necessary for built-in change.

And it is not just a matter of elevating the role of principals as instructional leaders and providing them with plenty of professional development. Ironically, as the role of the principal as a key change agent is being recognized at all levels, more and more expectations are being added, with little being taken away and little direct support. The principalship itself is in danger of sinking!

I say all this to indicate how complex the solution will be. It is structural and normative and implicates all levels of the system. The good news is that lack of knowledge about what to do is not the problem. The bad but nonetheless exciting news is that we are talking about complex, deep, systemic reform that has so far proven intractable. Even more exciting is that we are making progress on identifying and putting into place many of the key elements essential for lasting success.

Spotlight on Leadership and School Change makes a significant contribution to this movement toward deeper, lasting

improvement. It touches on critical issues—teacher collaboration, the role of accountability, the effort to reach out to every child and serve learners at all levels, and efforts to engage
the community. Each chapter represents a bite-sized chunk of
insight and offers practical strategies for using the ideas addressed. Time and again, the authors furnish new twists on
familiar topics, such as Elmore's notion that high-performing schools can learn more from low-performing schools than
from their high-performing peers, or Vaishnav's treatment of
the ins and outs of value-added assessment. Taken together,
these wide-ranging articles provide fresh and powerful insights about school reform, blending original and critical perspectives with an emphasis on practical results. This com-
pendium of brief and pointed essays is an invaluable resource
for anyone working in this complicated field.

REFERENCES

American Educational Research Association. (2007). *Tri-level improvement for literacy and numeracy in Ontario*. Chicago: Author.

Cole, P. (2004). *Professional development: A good way to avoid change*.
Melbourne, Australia: Centre for Strategic School Improvement.

Day, C., Sammons, P., Stobart, G., Kingston, A., & Qing, G. (2007).
Teachers matter. Berkshire, England: Open University Press.

Elmore, R. (2004). *School reform from the inside-out: Policy, practice,
and performance*. Cambridge, MA: Harvard University Press.

Fullan, M. (2007). *The new meaning of educational change* (4th ed.).
New York: Teachers College Press.

Fullan, M., Hill, P., & Crévola, C. (2006). *Breakthrough*. Thousand Oaks,
CA: Corwin.

Johnson, S. M. (2004). *Finders and keepers*. San Francisco: Jossey-Bass.

Introduction

by Nancy Walser and Caroline Chauncey

The advent of the federal No Child Left Behind Act caused many educators to focus primarily on test scores as the motivator and measure of reform. As could be predicted, a palpable backlash has emerged against using a singular standard for school success. With it comes the growing realization (or re-realization) that much, much more than testing goes into making a quality education possible for all students.

Scratch the surface of a "successful" school and you will find a web of interactions that are at the root of its success. Who is it that envisions, inspires, cajoles, and rallies all the various players in and around a school toward any improvement goal? Often it's a superintendent, a principal, a professor, a special teacher, or a parent. In a word, it's a leader.

It is not surprising, then, that in recent years, the *Harvard Education Letter* has published numerous stories highlighting ways that leadership has made a difference in schools. Twenty of these stories are presented here to form the latest volume in the *Harvard Education Letter* Spotlight Series. Whether the topic is teacher collaboration or parent involvement, special education or closing the achievement gap, these stories illustrate how education leaders—including some of the most renowned thinkers in their fields—have sought to effect change by bringing best practices to where students are: right in the classroom.

In Part I, our authors look at the role of leaders in perhaps their most critical job: improving instruction. Laura Pappano starts off by delving into the nuts and bolts of teacher collaboration, presenting several ways that principals are working with their staffs to structure productive collaboration for more effective instruction. Andreae Downs highlights the work being done in the Montgomery (Md.) County Public Schools to create a comprehensive teacher evaluation system based on teaching standards and student performance, and featuring peer review for novice and underperforming teachers. Downs also explores the use of online professional development with Harvard education professor Chris Dede. Robert Rothman writes about the visionary work of another Harvard education professor, Richard Elmore, to adapt the medical concept of "grand rounds" to the school setting in order to help superintendents dissect instructional problems and bolster their role as instructional leaders. Elmore ends the section with a cautionary essay on how much time in American classrooms is wasted on things other than instruction.

Part II takes a more detailed look at the assessment and accountability tools available to school leaders. The authors in this section examine a number of mechanisms or systems that involve staff in looking at student progress in new, more constructive ways. From the Data Wise improvement process developed at the Harvard Graduate School of Education to teacher-administered formative assessments to value-added assessments for tracking individual student growth, these tools are giving leaders concrete ways to plan and observe how their schools and students are achieving and, more importantly, to see exactly where more work needs to be done.

The authors in Part III examine issues related to diversity and achievement. As the experts in this area make clear, education leaders must understand the experiences that shape children's understanding and development in order to close the achievement gap and help all children succeed emotionally and academically in school. In a candid interview, Ronald Ferguson of Harvard's Achievement Gap Initiative lays out the research that points to some striking misperceptions about the black-white achievement gap, underscoring the urgent need to revisit teaching practices with these findings in mind. Three other authors in this section directly address the critical role of school leaders in minimizing the potential negative effects of homophobia, disability, race, and poverty in U.S. schools.

While leadership is critical, the very term implies the existence of others who will follow. Leaders need followers—or helpers in the very least. Part IV is comprised of several chapters focusing on how school leaders are rallying their communities to support students. Whether it means developing "assets" in youth, afterschool programs, or targeted parent engagement, savvy principals and other leaders are successfully recruiting help in achieving their goals from beyond the school yard and outside the school day.

Even with the best-intentioned, enlightened leadership, school change is neither easy nor quick, as the articles in Part V remind us. Mitch Bogen details the leadership necessary to bring reforms into the collective bargaining process, highlighting Denver's six-year campaign to get a pay-for-performance teacher contract. Leaders must also beware of stereotypes that can lull us into complacency, as Elmore emphasizes in a poignant essay comparing the sometimes meager improvement efforts in high-scoring suburban systems with the more robust efforts taking place in urban ones. Laura Cooper's essay on comprehensive high schools versus small schools illustrates that leaders may not necessarily want to "throw the baby out" in the name of reform. And, finally, Elmore's concluding essay, written with Liz City, is a must-read about patterns of change. It is bound to help leaders make sure that unrealistic expectations don't get in the way of progress.

If there is one constant in education, it is that change is inevitable. Ensuring that these changes are proactive, constructive, and in the best interests of all students is the hard work of leadership.

PART I

Instructional Improvement

CHAPTER 1

More Than "Making Nice"

Getting teachers to (truly) collaborate

by Laura Pappano

There was no yellow Post-It note, no collegial suggestion like, "Hey, I've tried these . . ." Newly hired French teacher Amy Moran merely found a stack of worksheets tossed on her desk by a colleague soon after she arrived at Westford Academy, a public high school in Westford, Mass.

With 10 years of teaching already under her belt, Moran had seen students benefit when teachers shared observations about strategies, lessons, and test results. The pile of worksheets made tangible what Moran already knew: She and her new colleague weren't working together. The two teachers gave students different tests and assessed the results separately. Who knew if their students were learning the same things? "To dump papers on a person's desk doesn't mean anything; it's not helpful," Moran recalls of the incident that occurred seven years ago.

It's hardly rare to find teachers who don't click. But such behavior—once considered an unfortunate personality conflict—is increasingly seen as a barrier to school success. Spurred by shifting teacher demographics and the drive for standards-based instruction, schools across the country are pressing teachers to take active roles in changing practice and to work together more effectively.

Principals in particular are responding by requiring teachers to participate in activities designed to encourage effective collaboration. They are going beyond simply providing common planning time, and setting specific tasks and goals that depend on collaboration, such as writing common assessments, identifying "power (essential) standards," and devising common curricula. They are also structuring meetings to help teachers stay on track and offering feedback:

- At Robert Adams Middle School in Holliston, Mass., new principal Jessica Huizenga revamped how teachers work. She provides common planning time for grade-level subject teachers to create and assess lessons together and demands that teachers submit written logs of their discussions as proof of real collaboration.
- As the founding principal of the three-year-old Chicago Academy High School, Brian Sims hired team-oriented teachers because, he says, "I wanted it to be a collaborative environment." He has assigned multiple teachers to teach different sections of the same course and requires them to create common curricula and assessments. To keep collaboration on track, Sims regularly attends teacher meetings.
- At Adlai Stevenson High School in Lincolnshire, Ill., principal Janet Gonzalez says the school's collaborative culture shows in its organizational chart. It's shaped like a bull's-eye, rather than a pyramid, and depicts a two-way flow of ideas between teachers and administrators. The key to success, she says, is the role of teacher leaders, who work with administrators to draft agendas for grade- and subject-level meetings and who keep talk focused on effective practices, rather than allowing griping or chit-chat.

The overall goal of creating a professional learning community requires a deep shift in teacher relations. Teachers are now asked to peel away facades, admit vulnerabilities, share precious insights, ask tough questions, compromise, and give colleagues real help—not just worksheets. Creating a safe and productive environment for these discussions is a new challenge for many principals and other school leaders.

"[Collaboration] is difficult in any workplace and it is probably more difficult in schools," says Richard DuFour, a Virginia-based educational consultant and coauthor of *Learning by Doing: A Handbook for Professional Learning Communities at Work.* "Teachers are used to total autonomy. Now they have to build consensus."

GENERATIONAL DIFFERENCES

Making teachers active team players, problem-solvers, and even innovators, however, requires a new approach to the profession. In 1975, when Dan C. Lortie famously characterized the work and rewards of the schoolteacher as largely individual, he was describing the norms of the era in which today's veteran teachers entered the profession. Susan Moore Johnson, professor of teaching and learning at the Harvard Graduate School of Education, says this isolated "egg-crate" structure reflects how schools grew—one classroom at a time—and an essential belief about the work itself.

Decades of research since Lortie's day, however, have linked strong collegial practices with school success—including a 1982 study by Judith Warren Little connecting regular talk about instruction, structured observations, and shared planning time as common to "high-success" schools. More recently, a new cohort of teachers has arrived from fields or with backgrounds steeped in team-oriented approaches. New teachers, says Johnson, "expect to work with other people. They do not expect to be left on their own."

Still, a 2004 study by Susan Kardos illustrates how difficult it has been for schools to make the shift from the egg-crate culture to a more collaborative one. Kardos found that nearly half of 486 first- and second-year public school teachers surveyed in California, Florida, Massachusetts, and Michigan planned and taught lessons alone.

Unfortunately, too many schools "are still structured for the retiring generation" and fail to push collaboration, says Johnson. But, she notes, pressure to show that *every* child is reaching standards has begun to make teamwork appealing. "Schools have had to face some data they have never had to look at before. It is disaggregated by subgroup, so they can't slide along based on the high performance of wealthy kids from the suburbs," says Johnson. "People within schools are realizing they need to work together, but [often] the time is not there and the skills are not available to them."

OVERCOMING TEACHER RESISTANCE IN ONE SCHOOL

When Huizenga, age 31 and a doctoral student, got her first principal's job at the Robert Adams Middle School and—steeped in the writings of DuFour and others—marched into a reasonably performing suburban school and announced her plan for teacher collaboration, she expected battles. In September she required that teachers jointly write new curricula and document collaboration in logs turned into her every two weeks. Each log entry included an outline of topics for teachers to talk about, with room to summarize the discussion. Topics to be covered included goals and objectives for the week or unit, common assessments and individual teacher assessments used, instructional strategies, and lesson design, as well as adjustments to instruction based on a shared evaluation of assessment results.

The teachers union at first balked, grieving the demands as a change in work conditions. But ultimately they relented.

GUIDELINES FOR COLLABORATION

Effective collaboration means moving teachers from broad aims (wanting all kids to learn) to specifics (learn what?), says Richard DuFour, educational consultant and coauthor of *Learning by Doing: A Handbook for Professional Learning Communities at Work.* His advice for making it work:

- Make student learning the center of collaboration: "Focus on the learner instead of the teacher."
- At the start, insist that teachers spell out rules for collaborating, including individual responsibilities and distribution of work.
- Set goals that can only be accomplished by working together. "Without a goal, you are not a team," says DuFour.
- Be certain goals are results oriented, not process oriented. For example, instead of deciding to do more hands-on labs, aim to raise fifth-grade science test scores by 10 percentage points, or to raise the percentage of As on final lab reports.
- Set a timeline and a means to measure progress. Administrators can help by creating a vehicle for teachers to check in and receive feedback.
- When conflicts arise, administrators must demand that collaborative work continue.

"I know they see me like this little Tasmanian devil, like a cyclone," she says of her faculty. "But I keep reinforcing that [collaboration] will make our work easier. This is not like the 1960s or 1970s teaching where we went on our guts," she says. "We will know exactly what kids know, what they need to know, and what we need to do to change our instruction so all kids are learning and successful."

Good idea, but tough to execute. One teacher at Huizenga's school, speaking on condition of anonymity, says that required sessions with a colleague have been frustrating, even painful. Assistant superintendent Timothy Cornely observes that some teachers always resist change. "Teachers also aren't used to problem-solving," he says. "They are used to, 'Here's the problem. Who do we tell?'"

However, sixth-grade science teacher Michelle Roy credits mandatory meetings with helping her and her two colleagues to focus on what works, even though the three of them "couldn't be more different people." Now they plan, discuss, and review labs together so if one approach yields clearer results for students, they will all teach the more effective lab— something that would have surfaced only by chance in the past.

"I was originally all about, 'This is my lab, this is my way of doing things,'" says Roy. She has learned to compromise and recently deferred when her colleagues both wanted to teach a particular lesson earlier in the year and she wanted to do it later. "I liked my way," Roy says, "but I said, 'Okay, let's do it. They are professionals.'"

In fact, teachers don't have to be friendly with each other to collaborate well, says DuFour. He stresses that collegial harmony should not be mistaken for collaboration, a more formal activity. "All teams have conflict," he notes. "Bad teams ignore it, while good teams work through it." (See "Guidelines for Collaboration," p. 11.)

LEADING THE WAY TO "DEVELOPMENTAL" PRACTICE

A 2006 study by W. David Stevens at the Consortium on Chicago School Research at the University of Chicago has

SUPPORTIVE VS. DEVELOPMENTAL PRACTICES

Typically, teachers help each other by using one of two types of collaborative practice. However, only developmental practices lead to lasting, systemic change.

Dimensions	Supportive Practices	Developmental Practices
Focus	Supporting routine tasks (i.e., sharing information about students or new ideas for classroom activities)	Improving instructional capacity (i.e., developing standards-based curricula or new interdisciplinary curricular units)
Context	Informal, individual, and group interactions (random conversation)	Formal, collective interactions (regular, structured meetings)
Prompts	Reactive (responding to immediate, pressing concerns)	Proactive (addressing systemic, general concerns)
Time Frame	Short-term solutions	Long-term projects
Type of Information Exchanged	Disconnected pieces of information about individual problems (spontaneous advice)	Connected sets of information about common problems (deliberate follow-up and monitoring)
Depth of Change	Isolated, corrective changes	Systemic, fundamental changes

Source: W.D. Stevens, with J. Kahne, "Professional Communities and Instructional Improvement Practices."

revealed barriers to meaningful collaboration, even when schools embrace the concept. The study identifies two kinds of collaborative practices. *Supportive practices* include teachers offering advice, suggesting approaches to tasks or concerns, and generally helping one another with daily classroom work. These typically occur informally and affect only one or a few teachers. *Developmental practices,* on the other hand, are interactions that spur improvements in overall instruction and change classroom practices. These require collective and structured efforts (see "Supportive vs. Developmental Practices," p. 13).

Teacher chit-chat about school "is not wasted time," Stevens says, "but it is not focused time, time that is used to sustain a larger improvement effort." He notes that the study of seven small schools in the Chicago High School Redesign Initiative revealed that discussions can easily get sidetracked and that real gains require a leader to take responsibility for setting goals and structuring collaborative teacher discussions.

One successful principal, for example, required teachers to create interim assessments based on college-readiness skills. Teachers reviewed test data together every two to three months, and together they made adjustments to keep kids on track. Another asked faculty members to list student performance goals by grade level. "The principal had the teachers think about what [they] expect freshmen to be able to do at the end of the school year [and also for] sophomores," and so on, says Stevens. Listing learning goals, he says, "helped teachers focus discussions on what they needed to do in the classroom to ensure students pick up those skills." Such goals, says Stevens, "force departments to work together."

At Westfield Academy, Moran's former colleagues have retired and she is now the French department veteran. Today, she and her colleagues regularly discuss program issues; for example, they recently decided students needed to speak more French in lower-level courses to prepare them for the demands of upper-level classes. "I really wonder if seven years ago we had been told to give a common assessment, if it would have changed the dynamic," says Moran. "We would have been forced to collaborate."

This chapter originally appeared in the March/April 2007 issue of the Harvard Education Letter.

FOR FURTHER INFORMATION

R. DuFour, R. DuFour, R. Eaker, and T. Many. *Learning by Doing: A Handbook for Professional Learning Communities at Work.* Bloomington, IN: Solution Tree, 2006.

S. Kardos. *Supporting and Sustaining New Teachers in School: The Importance of Professional Culture and Mentoring.* Cambridge, MA: Harvard University dissertation, 2004.

W.D. Stevens, with J. Kahne. "Professional Communities and Instructional Improvement Practices: A Study of Small High Schools in Chicago." Consortium on Chicago School Research at the University of Chicago, 2006. Available online at http://ccsr.uchicago.edu/publications/prof_comm_report.pdf

CHAPTER 2

Standards-Based Evaluation for Teachers

How one public school system links teacher performance, student outcomes, and professional growth

by Andreae Downs

E ric Luedtke recalls clearly his first evaluation as a student teacher. The only comments from the instructors who observed him were "Good job!" and "You did everything right."

"But I knew I had a lot to learn and a lot I could improve on," said Luedtke, who now teaches middle school social studies at the A. Mario Loiederman Middle School for the Creative and Performing Arts in Silver Spring, Md.

As accountability pressures on schools increase, teacher evaluation and supervision have come under new scrutiny. A growing body of research indicates that teacher quality has more impact on student achievement than any other factor. Given high turnover in the profession and the numbers of novice teachers streaming into the classroom, the challenge of ensuring high-quality instruction has taken on new urgency.

But the tools administrators are given for teacher evaluation are often antiquated or inadequate. Many principals still rely on an annual classroom observation, during which they match the teacher's behavior against a standard checklist. Was the assignment written on the board? Is student work displayed on the walls? Are students participating in structured activities? Many evaluation systems are not connected to clear standards of teacher performance, nor do they take into account how much students are actually learning. Moreover, many principals are expected to evaluate all their teachers every year—a Herculean task that does not recognize differences in needs and expectations for novice and veteran teachers. Perhaps most important, as Luedtke discovered, evaluation may not offer significant guidance in how to become a better teacher.

"Teacher evaluation in this country is generally abysmal," notes Julia Koppich, an educational consultant specializing in teacher quality and labor relations. "There is no time for principals to do proper evaluation, and many principals aren't trained to do evaluation well." Most evaluation systems, she adds, reflect a view of teaching as a set of codifiable skills or procedures. In this view, which originated in the "process-product" research of the 1970s, uniform methods are presumed to yield uniform results, regardless of the characteristics of student learners. As a result, evaluation rubrics emphasized teacher behavior, rather than student outcomes, and offered little opportunity for dialogue or problem-solving.

But at least one district has found a way to convert evaluation into a conversation about teaching and learning. Koppich points to the Montgomery County (Maryland) Public Schools' (MCPS) teacher evaluation system as an example of an approach that incorporates many of the key elements associated with effective teacher evaluation. Perhaps the most far-reaching overhaul of teacher assessment in the country, the Montgomery County model, known as the Professional Growth System, puts evaluation under the umbrella of staff development and uses it to continually increase teacher capacity. The system sets clear standards for quality teaching. Instead of using checklists, evaluators draw on a variety of sources, including written narratives, teacher portfolios, and student achievement results, to determine whether teachers are meeting those standards. It also establishes a two-tiered process for evaluation, depending on a teacher's level of experience and past evaluations. Overall, the Montgomery County approach to teacher evaluation resembles the standards-based, data-driven methods many districts now use to assess and boost student learning.

"I have not come across another district that's done something as intense and comprehensive as Montgomery County," says Koppich, who conducted a comprehensive evaluation of the Montgomery County Professional Growth System in 2004. "This is the best I've seen."

THE "SILVER BULLET"

The district changed its approach to teacher evaluation and education in 1999 with the arrival of Superintendent Jerry D. Weast, who argued that building staff capacity was the "silver bullet" for improving student outcomes. At the time, the district used a checklist for evaluation, a system that had been in place since the 1970s, according to Darlene Merry, associate superintendent in the Office of Organizational Development, which was established to coordinate the Professional Growth System. Under the guidance of Jon Saphier, president of Research for Better Teaching (RBT), an Acton, Mass.–based educational consulting firm, the administration and teachers union began to develop an evaluation system embedded in professional development.

To improve teacher evaluation, the district first adopted six performance standards based on the National Board for Professional Teaching Standards. These standards were incorporated into a two-tiered system for teacher assessment. New or struggling teachers face evaluation annually, while more experienced teachers are reviewed every three to five years. Each group has access to different resources and strategies for professional development to help them meet or exceed the standards. Merry likens this approach to a teacher's using differentiated instruction to accommodate students' varying needs. The district offers courses developed by RBT to establish a common framework for understanding skillful teaching and to train evaluators in observing and analyzing instruction.

Teacher evaluations include an examination of student results. But state and standardized tests are not the only measure of student learning. Formative assessments, such as assignments, classroom tests, or post-lesson questioning, are also part of the mix.

Novice teachers and teachers who fall short of meeting performance standards work with a Peer Assistance and Review (PAR) system modeled on one pioneered in the 1970s in Toledo, Ohio. A seasoned colleague serves as a consulting teacher in charge of several novice or struggling teachers. She acts as both an evaluator and a conduit for professional development, providing tips, support, model lessons, and other in- and out-of-class support.

THE POWER OF PEER REVIEW

Social studies teacher Luedtke, who is now in his second year of teaching, is grateful for his year of peer review. His consulting teacher observed him five or six times during his first year and suggested several areas where he could improve. Once he'd chosen an area to focus on, she would give him "specific tips, not generalized things that aren't that applicable," he recalls.

"A first-year teacher can feel alone in the classroom," says Luedtke. "To have a person come and give good advice helps alleviate that loneliness. And there's so much to learn! I don't know where I'd be without that support."

At the end of a novice teacher's first year, a PAR panel of teachers and administrators reviews the consulting teacher's recommendations and decides on retention. In the second year, the building principal evaluates the teacher. If the novice passes both evaluations, he or she is granted tenure.

For experienced or tenured teachers, the PAR process is triggered when a principal formally evaluates the teacher's performance as below standard. A consulting teacher will review the teacher's skills and determine whether the instructional problems identified are severe enough to warrant the teacher's inclusion in the PAR program. Underperforming teachers who are accepted into the program are then assigned a consulting teacher, who plans and implements an intensive yearlong program of intervention and support. At year's end, the consulting teacher also provides an independent evaluation, alongside the principal's formal evaluation, based on multiple observations and analysis of student results. The panel then makes a decision on retention.

Montgomery County Education Association head Bonnie Cullison sees peer review as a way to reinforce the value of teaching as a highly skilled vocation.

"For the last 18 years, progressive union leadership has said to our members, if we care about the profession, we can't say everyone can do it well," she says. "We need to help those who aren't being successful."

Merry notes that in the first four years of the peer-evaluation program, 163 new and veteran teachers were dismissed, were not renewed, or resigned, as opposed to one in the prior five years (out of about 10,000 teachers in the system). Nonetheless, over half of the teachers identified as struggling were able to improve their performance and get back on track.

HELPING SKILLED TEACHERS IMPROVE

Veteran teachers who meet or exceed the teaching standards are formally evaluated every three, four, or five years, depending on their experience. Instead of completing a checklist, principals write a narrative documenting a teacher's success or failure in meeting the district's teaching standards, based on their observations and on student performance.

Beth Daniels has taught science at Einstein High School in Montgomery County for the last nine years. In the days when her annual evaluation was based on a checklist, observers "would check off what they thought they saw, but didn't have to justify it," she says. "It really didn't tell me anything." The Professional Growth System "takes away the subjective parts," she says. "This is much more detailed, it's research-based, and based on student success. It's made us more reflective about what we've been doing."

Some principals experience the Montgomery County evaluation system as a logistical challenge. Writing up a single post-observation report can take anywhere from one to three hours. Daniel Shea, principal of Quince Orchard High School in Gaithersburg, Md., says that he is evaluating about a quarter of his staff—43 teachers—this year. "I have always worried about the capacity of administrators to do this as required," he says. "Can we do it within the limited number of hours there are in a day?" He says, however, that the evaluations and related professional development have meant a dramatic improvement in teaching.

Veteran teachers are also expected to set goals for a three-, four-, or five-year professional growth cycle, which they establish in conjunction with a school-based professional development teacher. The goals need to be aligned with both the school improvement plan and the teacher's own interests, and should be stated clearly enough that a principal can evaluate them, including targets for improving outcomes for student learning. Teachers, with guidance from administrators, also identify colleagues who can provide assistance and feedback.

"When [a plan] is more specific, we can help tailor resources to help with it," Shea notes. "We can also pair people who do something well with others who need [better] strategies."

TOWARD A CULTURE OF EVALUATION

Both teachers and administrators have found the MCPS teacher evaluation system helpful. In her 2004 evaluation report, Koppich found that large majorities of teachers at all grade levels found the system "highly effective," while 75 percent of administrators agreed that it "enabled me to be a better administrator." Koppich also cited more general results, including the use of multiple sources to assess student learning; increased use of data to drive instruction; and more frequent use of teaching strategies that research has shown to be effective. The school district's statisticians have documented increases in AP and SAT participation rates and above-average statewide test scores across racial and ethnic groups, which Merry cites as evidence of the success of the MCPS's efforts to improve teacher capacity. She notes that these changes occurred at a time when the student population in the district has become increasingly diverse, particularly in terms of class and language.

The next step in MCPS's efforts to link evaluation and improvement is to extend the process to principals, incorporating several of the same elements as the Professional Growth System. District administrators have developed six standards, based on the Interstate School Licensure Consortium, and created seven online lessons for principals and other administrators. RBT has trained about 30 staff members responsible for evaluating principals, and a review panel—a version of the Peer Assistance and Review for principals—has been formed. As with the teacher evaluations, student assessment results will be a critical part of the evaluation of principals' performance.

This chapter originally appeared in the March/April 2006 issue of the Harvard Education Letter.

FOR FURTHER INFORMATION

D. Lawrence. *The Toledo Plan: Peer Review, Peer Assistance; Practical Advice for Beginners.* Toledo, OH: Toledo Public Schools and Toledo Federation of Teachers, 2003. Available online at tft250.org.

J. Saphier and R. Gower. *The Skillful Teacher: Building Your Teaching Skills.* Acton, MA: Research for Better Teaching, 1997.

The Montgomery County Public Schools Professional Growth System Teacher Evaluation Handbook. Available online at mcps.k12.md.us/departments/personnel/teachereval/

CHAPTER 3

Online Professional Development for Teachers

Chris Dede discusses its strengths, forms, and future

As demands to improve teacher quality increase, online professional development programs have proliferated to meet a variety of needs. But little is known about best practices in the design and implementation of these programs. In Online Professional Development for Teachers: Emerging Models and Methods *(Harvard Education Press, 2006), Chris Dede, the Timothy E. Wirth Professor in Learning Technologies at the Harvard Graduate School of Education, and his colleagues analyze the strengths and limitations of selected models of online professional development in areas related to math, science, engineering, and technology.* Harvard Education Letter *contributor Andreae Downs spoke with Dede about issues in the design and implementation of online professional development.*

How does online professional development compare with face-to-face professional development?

It's a widely held misconception that any form of online learning is second best to any form of face-to-face learning.

What research shows us is that online learning and face-to-face learning complement each other in interesting ways. Some people who are silent in face-to-face professional development sessions find their voice in online interactions, for a variety of reasons. Online learning can also extend time, which is perhaps the most precious resource that teachers have, because it allows them to do professional development when they want, where they want. So it has some strengths that are a really good complement to face-to-face professional development.

But what online learning doesn't always provide is somebody right down the hall from you. Sometimes you want to get together in the teachers' lounge with somebody else who's going through the same experience. If professional development is all online, you lose some emotional and social immediacy. The best professional development is not face-to-face only or online only—it's both.

What's the best approach to combining online and face-to-face strategies?

I don't think that it chunks into topic areas so that, for instance, you would learn subject content face-to-face and pedagogy online, or vice versa. I think it's more that face-to-face learning offers a kind of immediacy, especially on the emotional and social level, that builds up intensity, and that online offers a broader set of resources, more flexibility in terms of time, and a chance for people who aren't good face-to-face to find their voice.

An important advantage of online professional development is the lower costs associated with scaling up. Scalability is very important in professional development, because to change the culture or the policies of an organization, the processes by which teaching and learning take place, a critical mass of teachers has to be willing to take the leap to a different model. If it's just a few teachers doing things in a new way, it's not likely to be very successful, because the whole system is set up to work in the traditional fashion. So doing professional development at scale to be transformative is really an important strategy.

Teaching is such a face-to-face profession—how can online learning help to transform that kind of culture?

We don't have any reason to believe that face-to-face professional development is automatically better at helping teachers transform their roles and practices than online learning is. What we do know is that transformation is an intellectual, emotional, and social process, and that having strong support on all three dimensions is necessary, whether it's online or face-to-face.

Online professional development lends itself to kinds of learning that are more powerful for many people than face-to-face learning. It gives people a chance to make sure they have the meaning of what they're reading or listening to, and then to compose their response. Also, people who are shy, who are reluctant to share their thinking about new ideas in front of their peers, often feel disinhibited online. It's not quite as intense an experience as face-to-face learning. So when we study participation patterns, we see much richer participation patterns online, often more thoughtful participation patterns than we see face-to-face. And for transformational change, that's very important.

What guidance might you provide to administrators selecting online professional development programs?

I think the first thing for an administrator to do is a needs assessment of their own professional development: where it is strong; where they are lacking local expertise or local resources, and how to bring that in from the outside; what kinds of learning their teachers seem to enjoy most. With that kind of needs assessment, then it's possible to look at what's available online and find a good match: a program that builds on the strengths of what they already have, that's consistent with their goals, and that's affordable.

How did you choose the models featured in your book?

I selected 10 high-quality models that had been around long enough that they had a track record, in terms of effectiveness data, and that were quite different from one another, in terms of the knowledge and skills being taught, the technologies used, and the audience (see "10 Exemplary Models," p. 29). I wanted to get a sense of the complete design space within which people are doing online teacher professional development.

Professional development is suited to a wide range of ways of helping teachers. For instance, teachers may feel they were inadequately prepared in terms of their subject matter. Or they may feel that they know the content well, but perhaps they've changed careers and not really had the kinds of pedagogical preparation that they would like. New teachers may struggle with classroom management and with basic teaching skills like creating lesson plans or individualized education programs (IEPs). Experienced teachers may wish to move into more of a leadership role. We tried to pick models that addressed all of these dimensions.

What are some of the promising aspects of the models that you looked at?

One model that we looked at is called EdTech Leaders Online. This is a suite of courses from the Educational Development Center (EDC) that trains people from the district to teach online workshops to their colleagues. So in a sense, EDC is training the trainers for online teacher professional development. Districts see it as a way of building their own

10 EXEMPLARY MODELS

The 10 models for online teacher professional development programs identified as exemplary by Chris Dede and his colleagues at the Harvard Graduate School of Education include:

- e-Mentoring for Student Success, ementoring.mspnet.org
- EdTech Leaders Online, www.edtechleaders.org
- Learning to Teach with Technology Studio, ltts.indiana.edu
- Milwaukee Public Schools Professional Support Portal, mpsportal.milwaukee.k12.wi.us/portal/server.pt
- Online Masters in Science Education, scienceonline.terc.edu
- PBS TeacherLine and Seeing Math, teacherline.pbs.org/teacherline, seeingmath.concord.org/
- Quest Atlantis, atlantis.crlt.indiana.edu
- Seminars on Science, learn.amnh.org
- Teachers' Domain, www.teachersdomain.org
- WIDE World, wideworld.pz.harvard.edu

capacity, rather than having to pay an outside group indefinitely for a service. The leadership dimension to it, too, is something that teachers value.

Another model is the Harvard Graduate School of Education's WIDE World model. It builds on Teaching for Understanding, an instructional approach that can improve many different kinds of learning. There are a relatively small number of people who understand it deeply. If you were head of a district and you wanted a detailed exposure to Teaching for Understanding, it might be quite difficult to accomplish that face-to-face. But it's quite easy to accomplish that using

WIDE World. Studying WIDE World is helping us to understand how to incorporate a new pedagogy across distance.

The Milwaukee Portal is not only for professional development but also day-to-day work of all types: attendance, IEPs, lesson planning. The original impetus was to provide a supportive place online to help new teachers feel empowered. It expanded to include all teachers and all kinds of district initiatives. It's been a very interesting experiment in trying to give teachers tools that help to make them more effective.

Some of our model projects are from places that have a lot of digital resources: museums or television stations. There they are taking an existing suite of resources and helping teachers find the material they need and use it effectively within a classroom setting.

What do you see as the next steps in online professional development?

We need to develop a research agenda for online teacher professional development—its effectiveness, its design, the promise of new media. Almost any aspect of an online professional development model is understudied right now, relative to what we know about face-to-face professional development.

What we're seeing are first-generation models that largely came out of the minds of designers. I'm hoping people will start thinking about what second-generation models should look like. Those models, presumably, will have much more input from teachers, who can provide valuable suggestions about how to make the models more effective. This is a natural evolution that will really increase both the appeal and the impact of online teacher professional development.

This chapter originally appeared in the July/August 2006 issue of the Harvard Education Letter.

CHAPTER 4

R$_X$ for a Profession

**The Connecticut Superintendents' Network
uses a "medical rounds" model to discuss
teaching and learning**

by Robert Rothman

L ike many school administrators, Mary Conway, superintendent of the Plainfield (Conn.) School District, used to devote the bulk of her time and energy to the routine operations of her 3,000-pupil rural district. Over the past four years, though, she and her leadership team have begun to turn their focus from bus schedules and meal programs to topics like student reading performance. Conway attributes this shift in perspective to her participation in the Connecticut Superintendents' Network, a group of two dozen administrators from urban, rural, and suburban districts throughout the state who meet monthly to discuss research, visit classrooms, and reflect on their role as superintendents in supporting instructional improvement.

The network was founded in 2001 by Richard F. Elmore, a professor of educational leadership at the Harvard Graduate School of Education, and Andrew Lachman, the executive director of the Connecticut Center for School Change. Both had been involved with New York City's Community School District #2 in the 1990s, when the district underwent a nationally recognized reform effort focused intensively on instructional improvement. (Elmore had conducted a long-term study of District #2, and Lachman had served as executive assistant to District #2's superintendent, Anthony Alvarado.) Lachman and Elmore sought to form a statewide network to support the efforts of high-level administrators to improve instruction in their districts.

The network is aimed at turning superintendents' gaze to what happens in classrooms and their role in improving it, says Lachman—a view that cuts against the conventional view of the superintendency as a managerial role far removed from the classroom. "From the beginning, the focus has been on the connection to instructional improvement," he says. "Everything else is out of bounds."

The popularity of the network suggests that the idea meets a critical need. Last year, the group added a second cohort of superintendents, expanding from its original group of 12, and more leaders have expressed interest in joining.

"I work 16 hours a day and go from meeting to meeting, mostly on quotidian stuff," says Joshua Starr, superintendent of the Stamford Public Schools, who joined the network last year. "At least once a month, I know I will sit down with colleagues and take a deep breath and take the long view. I like that."

"FORCING QUESTIONS"

At the heart of the network are monthly classroom visits, modeled on physicians' use of medical rounds. In teaching hospitals, students and senior physicians visit patients and then review cases together. In addition, physicians regularly conduct "grand rounds," in which practitioners from various specialties visit patients and analyze specific cases.

Elmore says he began to understand the power of the medical rounds model for training doctors—and its potential application to working with school administrators—when he was diagnosed with a heart ailment about 10 years ago. Both types of rounds, he says, have the advantage of "forcing questions . . . about the social organization of practice: Who knows what? How does knowledge get organized and transmitted?"

The network's "rounds" follow a typical pattern. First, the host superintendent presents a "workup" of an instructional problem to the network, drawing on performance data, classroom work and observations, and the superintendent's own reflections. The following month, the superintendents visit a school in the district. They break into groups of three or four to observe classrooms, using a simple protocol (see "Questions for Classroom Observation," p. 35), then reconvene for a short debriefing session before leaving the school. The following month, the superintendents meet to discuss their observations, with the goal of developing a plan for the next level of work in the district.

For example, one high-poverty, high-minority district was having little success introducing a high-level literacy curriculum that involved intensive work with small groups of students. The network's observations and discussions uncovered the fact that teachers were having difficulty engaging the whole class. Students were highly engaged when the teacher was working directly with them. But other students were staring into space or engaged in unproductive work. In another district, which was experiencing a substantial achievement gap between white and African American students, the network found that only a handful of students, all white, were responding to teachers' questions. In each case, the district ensured that teachers became aware of these patterns of interaction and provided professional development to help them learn new strategies.

Elmore and others involved in the network acknowledge that they have not solved all the problems the group has addressed. They stress that the network's most important accomplishment has been to help district leaders perceive themselves as instructional leaders, rather than as managers who leave instructional decisions to others. Lachman points out that the network began meeting as a seminar, and that many superintendents were reluctant to take part in school visits at first. "It took us almost a year to convince them to leave the comfort of the conference table and go into a school," he recalls. "Once they did it, they converted to walkthroughs."

"Embedding our discussions in practice was a catalyst for our learning," agrees Bob Villanova, superintendent of the Farmington Public Schools.

COMMONALITY IN VARIABILITY

One key insight that emerged was the remarkable consistency of instructional problems across the state. Although the districts represented are demographically dissimilar and show varying levels of student performance, the superintendents found the same pattern across districts: a few classrooms with high-level instruction, but many more in which students "are not sufficiently challenged," according to Patrick Proctor, superintendent of the Wethersfield Public Schools. "There is a large amount of variability from classroom to classroom and school to school. We noted that everywhere we've been."

This commonality of experience means that network leaders can benefit from one another's wisdom, notes Doris J. Kurtz, superintendent of the New Britain Public Schools. "The lack of rigor in classrooms is universal," she says. "It's an education problem, not an urban problem."

Elmore points out that the group has found very few examples of inadequate teaching. "These are not mediocre teachers," he notes. "[But] they are not at the level we are asking

QUESTIONS FOR CLASSROOM OBSERVATION

The protocol below is used by the Connecticut Superintendents' Network. As in medical rounds, the focus is on evidence, not interpretation.

In each classroom observe carefully; note down what you see and hear.

1. What is the teacher doing?
2. What is the teacher saying and to whom?
3. What are the students doing?
4. What are the students saying and to whom?
5. What kind of student work is in view? Where?
6. What evidence shows that instruction is informed by pre-lesson student performance diagnostic data?
7. What evidence exists that instruction is adjusted to reflect the level of student skill and knowledge?

them to work." He stresses that since the network is not aimed at evaluating teachers, its focus is on the practice, not the practitioner.

Accordingly, the superintendents have begun to take note of the characteristics of effective teaching. For instance, they have found that successful classrooms are ones in which students spend relatively more time talking, and teachers less. Network members have also observed that challenging assignments are more likely to produce high-quality learning. And they note that schools are most effective when the adults in the building have opportunities to work together and reflect on their practice.

"CREATING AN ALTERNATIVE CULTURE"

Based on their experience with the network, many members have created their own versions of it within their districts. For example, the leadership team of the Farmington Public Schools conducts school visits and holds focused discussions around issues of teaching and learning, according to Villanova. "We replicated the network at our local site level," he says. "Every six weeks, the leadership team visits schools and talks about what we have seen and how we can become more supportive of classroom teachers."

Superintendents have also convinced principals to make classroom work more visible. In one school, for example, the principal asked every teacher to submit every student work sample for a given week, then asked them to meet in the auditorium, look at the samples, and classify them according to Benjamin Bloom's taxonomy of educational objectives. "The result was exactly what you'd predict from [the Third International Mathematics and Science Study]," says Elmore. "Eighty percent of the work was procedural and factual recall. Almost none was higher-level understanding. That got the teachers' attention."

In 2005, Elmore transferred the network idea to Cambridge, Mass., at the request of Superintendent Thomas Fowler-Finn, who had heard about the Connecticut project. The Cambridge network includes the superintendent, representatives of the central office, all of the principals, and the head of the local teachers union. Elmore says the diversity in roles within the Cambridge network has proven to be a plus. "Having central office staff—the superintendent, the deputy, and instructional support—in school visits and analysis makes the possibility of connections between classroom-level work, school-level work, and district-level work more evident," he says.

He also notes that the Cambridge group has committed itself to documenting how districts have changed practice as a result of the network activities. Such documentation was not built into the Connecticut network, he points out. "It's a work in progress," Elmore says. "We're trying to figure out how to do it."

In all these ventures, Elmore acknowledges, the goal is to create a cadre of education professionals who understand what high-quality instruction looks like and their role in supporting it. "Education is a profession without a practice," he says. "It does not have an agreed-upon core body of knowledge that is transmissible from one body to another."

In redefining the role of the superintendent as instructional leader, "we're creating an alternative culture and trying to displace the existing culture," he continues. "That's like moving graveyards. It's not attractive or easy work."

This chapter originally appeared in the May/June 2006 issue of the Harvard Education Letter.

FOR FURTHER INFORMATION

R.F. Elmore. *School Reform from the Inside Out*. Cambridge, MA: Harvard Education Press, 2004.

R.F. Elmore and D. Burney. *Investing in Teacher Learning: Staff Development and Instructional Improvement in Community School District #2, New York City*. New York: National Commission on Teaching & America's Future, Consortium on Policy and Education, 1997.

The Superintendents' Network, Connecticut Center for School Change, 151 New Park Avenue, Suite 203, Hartford, CT 06106. ctschoolchange. org/work_supernet.htm

CHAPTER 5

Three Thousand Missing Hours

Where does the instructional time go?

by Richard F. Elmore

One of the most remarkable things about American classrooms is how little real teaching goes on there. Over the past five years or so, I have spent at least three or four days a month in schools studying the relationship between classroom practice and school organization. I observe classrooms at all levels—primary, middle, and secondary grades—and in all subjects. One of the most striking patterns to emerge is that teachers spend a great deal of classroom time getting ready to teach, reviewing and reteaching things that have already been taught, giving instructions to students, overseeing student seatwork, orchestrating administrative tasks, listening to announcements on the intercom, or presiding over dead air—and relatively little time actually teaching new content.

When my fellow researchers and I code our observations for teaching new content, it is not unusual to find that it occupies somewhere between zero and 40 percent of scheduled instructional time. Over the course of a typical 180-day school year with a 6-hour day (subtracting an hour for programmed noninstructional time), this means that a student might lose somewhere between 200 and 300 hours of instruction per year (40 to 60 days) to just the daily friction of classroom processes.

Let's compare two middle-grade math lessons taken from the Third International Mathematics and Science Study (TIMSS). The first, in a typical American classroom, begins with a problem-by-problem homework review focused on procedure and factual recall. It proceeds to a teacher-directed lesson with no discernible connection to the homework, and ends with a long period of seatwork focused on tomorrow's homework. There are probably fewer than 15 minutes of instruction in new content in a 55-minute class.

The second lesson takes place in a Japanese classroom. The teacher begins with a brief introduction to the problem of the day including a short connection to the previous day's work, followed by a combination of individual seatwork, pair work, and group problem-solving, which in turn is followed by students presenting their work and a discussion among the teacher and students of what the students have produced. All of the content is new. The class moves to another problem; the process is the same.

When American educators watch these two lessons they are shocked by the difference: Students in the Japanese lesson are fully engaged in new content for the entire class, while in the American lesson it is difficult to discern what the new content actually is, much less how much time is dedicated to it. Observers invariably comment on how respectful and comfortable students and teachers are with each other in the Japanese lesson, and how distant and incoherent the discourse is in the American classroom. They see that meaningful work produces meaningful discourse and meaningful results.

The assumption that when teachers are teaching, students are learning is, of course, conditional on the quality of instruction. Recent research shows that low-quality teaching results in disengagement by students. A recent article by Sam Intrator describes the "flavors of disengagement" among students in high school classrooms: "slow time" (daydreaming); "lost time" (waiting for class to end); "fake time" (pretending to pay attention); "worry time" (fretting over nonacademic matters); and "play time" (socializing). My calculus of lost instructional time does not even include these categories.

In all my hours in the classroom, I have yet to see a student refuse to engage in meaningful academic work. A good deal of what American students are asked to do with their time in school, however, does not meet this standard.

TIME LOST TO TESTING

Then there is testing. State tests take at least two full days of instructional time for each student, and usually more. In addition, many local districts routinely engage in "benchmark" testing to diagnose how students are doing between state testing periods. These are often given in at least three subjects—reading/writing/English language arts, mathematics, and history/social studies—and each test takes at least half a day. At a minimum, then, state and district tests account for 10 to 18 hours per year (roughly 2 to 4 days) of lost instructional time.

What about test prep? Students ranked proficient or above will often receive a day or two of instruction on the test content and format; lower-scoring students usually receive significantly more. It is not unusual, for example, for schools to program an hour or so of instruction during the school day and an hour or so after school over at least a month for students at risk of failing. Many teachers also spend a week of review—scripted walk-throughs of test content and format—to prepare students for district-administered benchmark tests. So a student might spend as little as 5 hours or as much as 60 hours per year (1 to 12 days) in test prep.

THE END-OF-YEAR LETDOWN

Finally, in American schools instruction in new content basically grinds to a halt anywhere from a month to two weeks before the end of the school year. This is the period when many schools engage in field trips and off-site activities. In the upper grades, there is often a long period of preparation for final exams. In affluent schools, students begin taking Advanced Placement examinations weeks before the end of school, preceded by a week to a month of review. Once the exams are administered, there is basically no further instruction. The end-of-year letdown accounts for anywhere from 30 to 75 hours per year (6 to 15 days) of lost instructional time.

Taking all these factors into account, a conservative estimate would indicate that American students lose at least 245 to 450 hours (approximately 50 to 90 days) of instruction in new content per year. Over the course of 12 years, this amounts to between 3,000 and 5,400 hours (600 to 1,100 days, or somewhere between *3 and 6 full years*) of lost instruction in new content. It should not surprise us, then, that American students' performance on international tests lags behind that of students in other industrialized countries by two years or more in the middle grades, a gap that only increases in the upper grades. Numbers like these make me extremely skeptical of proposals to lengthen the school day and year, which would amount to pouring more water into a very leaky bucket.

TEACHING VS. RETEACHING

Critics may take issue with "instruction in new content" as the criterion for effective use of instructional time. Aren't review and reteaching just as important as instruction in new content? Isn't test preparation a valid form of instruction? Observing classrooms has made me deeply skeptical on both these questions. Most review and reteaching is a consequence of a hopelessly fragmented and disorganized curriculum, often coupled with extremely weak teaching in the first place. Most test prep is low-level instruction with no discernible curricular design. I see almost no evidence that time spent testing delivers anything like the value it extracts from instruction.

In a number of other industrialized countries (such as Japan, Finland, and The Netherlands), teachers base their instruction on a strong, parsimonious curriculum designed around clear and accessible standards for student learning. In high-performing countries like these, the time students spend taking tests is seen as a dead loss to instruction, and as such is carefully weighed against the benefits of more teaching and more active student engagement in learning. In America, testing is viewed as a free good by whoever proposes it, with no clear standard for controlling its costs to instruction.

I am increasingly persuaded that the use of time in classrooms is a measure of the respect adults have for the role of learning in the lives of students. I have also become aware of how profoundly disrespectful schools, and the people who work in them, are of the time and effort they extract from the lives of students and their families, without regard to the value this time adds to students' learning and development. The way schools use time is a product of many choices: the way the curriculum is designed, the way the school day is organized, the demands of testing on instructional time, the daily routines that teachers establish in their classrooms, and the attention, or lack thereof, to students' classroom experiences by adults in schools. It would be an enormous step forward if adults in schools treated the time that children and their families give to schools as a precious gift rather than an

PART II

Assessment and Accountability

CHAPTER 6

The "Data Wise" Improvement Process

Eight steps for using test data to improve teaching and learning

by Kathryn Parker Boudett, Elizabeth A. City, and Richard J. Murnane

The package containing data from last spring's mandatory state exam landed with a thud on principal Roger Bolton's desk. The local newspaper had already published an article listing Franklin High as a school "in need of improvement." Now this package from the state offered the gory details. Roger had five years of packages like this one, sharing shelf space with binders and boxes filled with results from the other assessments required by the district and state. The sheer mass of paper was overwhelming. Roger wanted to believe that there was something his faculty could learn from all these numbers that would help them increase student learning. But he didn't know where to start.

School leaders across the nation share Roger's frustration. The barriers to constructive, regular use of student assessment data to improve instruction can seem insurmountable. There is just so much data. Where do you start? How do you make time for the work? How do you build your faculty's skill in interpreting data sensibly? How do you build a culture that focuses on improvement, not blame? How do you maintain momentum in the face of all the other demands at your school?

Our group of faculty and doctoral students at the Harvard Graduate School of Education and school leaders from three Boston public schools worked together for over two years to figure out what school leaders need to know and do to ensure that the piles of student assessment results landing on their desks are used to improve student learning in their schools. We have found that organizing the work of instructional improvement around a process that has specific, manageable steps helps educators build confidence and skill in using data. After much discussion, we settled on a process that includes eight distinct steps school leaders can take to use their student assessment data effectively, and organized these steps into three phases: Prepare, Inquire, and Act.

The "Data Wise" Improvement Process graphic shown opposite illustrates the cyclical nature of this work. Initially, schools *prepare* for the work by establishing a foundation for learning from student assessment results. Schools then *inquire*—look for patterns in the data that indicate shortcomings in teaching and learning—and subsequently *act* on what they learn by designing and implementing instructional improvements. Schools can then cycle back through inquiry and further action in a process of ongoing improvement. In the brief overview below, we outline the steps in what can be both a messy and ultimately satisfying undertaking. (To learn what districts can do to support this work, see "The 'Data Wise' District," p. 51.)

STEP 1. ORGANIZING FOR COLLABORATIVE WORK

Ongoing conversations around data are an important way to increase staff capacity to both understand and carry out

school improvement work. School leaders who regularly engage their faculties in meaningful discussions of assessment results and other student data often describe themselves as being committed to building a "data culture" or "culture of inquiry." To build this kind of culture, your school will need to establish a data team to handle the technical and organizational aspects of the work, including compiling an inventory of data from various sources and managing this information. You will also want to establish team structures and schedules that enable collaborative work among faculty members, and engage in careful planning and facilitation to ensure that collaborative work is productive. Because looking deeply at student performance and teaching practice can be uncomfortable at first, you may find that using formal protocols to structure group discussions can be quite helpful.

STEP 2: BUILDING ASSESSMENT LITERACY

When you look through the assessment reports for your school, it can sometimes feel as if they are written in a different language. So many terms, so many caveats, so many footnotes! As a school leader, how can you help your faculty begin to make sense of it all? An essential step in the "Prepare" phase is to help your faculty develop assessment literacy. To interpret score reports, it helps to understand the different types of assessments and the various scales that are used. To appreciate what inferences may be drawn from these reports and which differences in outcomes are meaningful, familiarity with key concepts such as reliability, validity, measurement error, and sampling error can really help. It is also important to have a candid discussion with your faculty about why "gaming the system" by teaching to the test may not serve students well.

STEP 3: CREATING A DATA OVERVIEW

As you move into the "Inquiry" phase of the process, a good starting place is to have your data team create graphic displays of your standardized test results. Schools often receive assessment reports in a format that can be quite overwhelming. With a modest investment in learning technical skills, your data team can repackage these results to make it easier for your faculty to see patterns in the data. As a school leader, you can then engage your teachers and administrators in constructive conversations about what they see in the data overview. Again, using protocols to structure conversations can help ensure that these discussions are productive.

THE "DATA WISE" DISTRICT

What can district administrators do to support schools in becoming "data wise"?

1. Set Up a Data System

Whether the district creates its own system or purchases a software program, administrators must consider:

- What data to include
- How to organize it and update it regularly
- Computational power vs. ease of use
- How to balance access and confidentiality

2. Create Incentives

One incentive is to require that school improvement plans be based on student assessment results. If schools with strong improvement plans and proven results are granted more autonomy, this can motivate school teams to do the analysis work well.

3. Support New Skills

School staffs will need professional development to support a variety of skills:

- How to interpret and use assessment data
- How to access data and create graphic displays
- How to participate productively in group discussions
- How to develop, implement, and assess action plans

4. Find the Time

Teachers need time to work together in order to learn and implement these new skills. Options can include:

- Scheduling a weekly early release day
- Paying substitutes to cover classes
- Compensating teachers for extra time

5. Model the Work

District leaders can also model the "Data Wise" Improvement Process. This may be new and challenging work for most members of the central office team, but it sends a strong message to the district's schools.

STEP 4: DIGGING INTO STUDENT DATA

Once your faculty has discussed the data overview, it is time to dig into student data to identify a "learner-centered problem"—a problem of understanding or skill that is common to many students and underlies their performance on assessments. In this step of the process, you may look deeply into the data sources you investigated for your data overview. You will also go on to investigate other data sources to look for patterns or inconsistencies (see "Triangulating Data," p. 53). The process of digging into data can deepen your faculty's understanding of student performance, help you move past "stuck points" ("We're teaching it, but they're not getting it!"), and allow you to come to a shared understanding of the skills or knowledge around which your students need the most support.

STEP 5: EXAMINING INSTRUCTION

In order to solve your learner-centered problem, it is important at this stage to reframe it as a "problem of practice" that your faculty will tackle. Now the challenge is to develop a shared understanding of what effective instruction around this issue would look like. School leaders can help teachers become skilled at examining practice, articulating what is actually happening in classrooms, and comparing it to the kind of instruction that is needed.

STEP 6: DEVELOPING AN ACTION PLAN

Solutions at last! It may seem as though you have to work through a large number of steps before deciding what to do about the issues suggested by your data. But because of the careful work you have done so far, the remaining steps will go more smoothly. In this first step of the "Act" phase of the work, you begin by deciding on an instructional strat-

"TRIANGULATING DATA":
DIGGING DEEPER INTO MULTIPLE SOURCES

A central premise of the "Data Wise" Improvement Process is that it is important to examine a wide range of data, not just results from standardized tests. Many schools use analysis of individual test items as a starting point in the effort to understand student thinking. In item analysis, you first look at test items in groups by content (such as geometry) or type (such as multiple choice) to see if there are gaps in specific skills. Then you look for patterns across groups of similar items. Finally, you look more closely at individual test items to hypothesize why students responded to certain questions in particular ways.

Schools can then "triangulate" their findings by using multiple data sources to illuminate, confirm, or dispute their initial hypotheses. Sources may include classroom projects, lab reports, reading journals, unit tests, homework, or teacher observations. Another rich source of data is the students themselves. Conducting focus groups with students to talk about their thinking can be very helpful.

When triangulating data, prepare to be surprised. It is important to approach the process with the idea that you will find something new. When the goal is merely to confirm a hypothesis, only particular kinds of data tend to be looked at and the work often stops when the hypothesis is confirmed. Instead, look for and embrace unexpected trends and leads.

egy that will solve the problem of practice you identified. You then work collaboratively to describe what this strategy will look like when implemented in classrooms. Then it is time to put the plan down on paper. By documenting team members' roles and responsibilities, you build internal accountability. By identifying the professional development and instruction your team will need and including it in your action plan, you let teachers know they will be supported every step of the way.

STEP 7: PLANNING TO ASSESS PROGRESS

Before implementing your plan, you need to figure out how you will measure its success. Too often, educators skip this step and find themselves deep into implementation without a clear sense of how they will assess progress. As a school leader, you can help your school decide in advance what short-, medium-, and long-term data you will gather and how you will gather it. You can then work together to set clear short-, medium-, and long-term goals for student improvement.

STEP 8: ACTING AND ASSESSING

Your school team worked hard to put their action plan ideas down on paper. Now that it is time to bring the ideas up off the paper, four questions can guide your work as a school leader: Are we all on the same page? Are we doing what we said we'd do? Are our students learning more? Where do we go from here? Implementation of the action plan can be like conducting an experiment in which you test your theories of how instructional strategies lead to student learning.

We made a very conscious decision to draw the "Data Wise" Improvement Process as an arrow curving back on itself. Once you get to the "end" of the "Act" phase, you continue to repeat the cycle with further inquiry. As the practice of using a structured approach to improving instruction be-comes ingrained, you may find it easier to know what ques-tions to ask, how to examine the data, and how to support teachers and students. You will also be able to go deeper into the work, asking tougher questions, setting higher goals, and involving more people in using data wisely.

This chapter originally appeared in the January/February 2006 issue of the Harvard Education Letter.

FOR FURTHER INFORMATION

R.A. Heifetz and D.L. Laurie. "The Work of Leadership." *Harvard Business Review* (January–February 1997): 124–134.

J.P. McDonald, N. Mohr, A. Dichter, and E.C. McDonald. *The Power of Protocols: An Educator's Guide to Better Practice.* New York: Teachers College Press, 2003.

Assessment Glossary, National Center for Research on Evaluation, Standards, and Student Testing (CRESST). Available online at http://cresst96.cse.ucla.edu/CRESST/pages/glossary.htm.

M. Schmoker. "First Things First: Demystifying Data Analysis." *Educational Leadership* 60, no. 5 (2003): 22–24.

CHAPTER 7

(In)formative Assessments

**New tests and activities can help teachers
guide student learning**

by Robert Rothman

Although many teachers in the No Child Left Behind (NCLB) era complain that students take too many tests, teachers at the John D. Philbrick Elementary School in Boston eagerly signed on last year to give students six more tests a year. The tests, known as Formative Assessments of Student Thinking in Reading, or FAST-R, are short multiple-choice quizzes that probe key reading skills. The tests are designed so that teachers can make adjustments to their instruction based on students' answers.

With FAST-R "we get concrete, helpful information on students very quickly," says Steve Zrike, Philbrick's principal.

Now used in 46 schools in Boston, FAST-R is part of a rapidly growing nationwide effort to implement so-called formative assessments—tests that can inform instruction through timely feedback. (By contrast, end-of-term tests and standards-based accountability tests are called summative assessments because they provide a summary of what students have learned.) Interest in formative assessment is fueled by the growing pressure to raise student achievement. Because the state tests on which schools will be judged under NCLB are typically administered at the end of the academic year, educators like Zrike are eager for information that can help them predict whether students are on track toward meeting proficiency goals and then intervene appropriately.

A strong body of evidence indicates that formative assessment, done properly, can generate dramatic improvements in teaching and learning. But some experts warn that many of the instruments marketed as formative assessments are in effect summative tests in disguise. At best such tests provide little useful information to classroom teachers; at worst they can narrow the curriculum and exacerbate the negative effects of teaching to the test, says Lorrie A. Shepard, dean of the School of Education at the University of Colorado at Boulder.

"If all the test produces is a predictive score, or tells you which students to be anxious about, it's a waste of money," she says. True formative assessments, she says, tell teachers "what it is the students aren't understanding."

TASTING THE SOUP

With the proliferation of so many instruments, it's not surprising that many educators find the distinction between formative and summative assessment confusing (see "Three Types of Assessment," p. 59). Paul Black, coauthor of a landmark 1998 study on the topic, once described the difference by saying that formative assessment is when the chef tastes the soup; summative assessment is when the customer tastes the soup. As his remark implies, the effectiveness of the process depends not only on the data sampled, but the timeliness of the feedback and how the "chefs"—not only teachers but the students themselves—use it.

In the 1998 study, Black and Dylan Wiliam, both of Kings College, London, examined some 250 studies from around the world and found that the use of formative assessment tech-

THREE TYPES OF ASSESSMENT

	Summative	*Benchmark*	*Formative*
Key Question	*Do* you understand? (yes or no)	Is the class on track for proficiency?	*What* do you understand?
When Asked	End of unit/term/year	6–10 times per year	Ongoing
Timing of Results	After instruction ends	Slight delay	Immediate

niques produced significant accelerations in learning. Students in classes using this approach gained a year's worth of learning in six or seven months. The method appeared particularly effective for low-performing pupils. As a result, formative assessment was found to narrow achievement gaps while it raised achievement overall.

"We know of no other way of raising [achievement] standards," the authors conclude, "for which such a strong prima facie case can be made on the basis of evidence of such large learning gains."

While skilled teachers may be adept at checking for comprehension, identifying misunderstandings, and adjusting instruction accordingly, the authors cited ample research showing the pervasiveness of ineffective or counterproductive assessment techniques in the classroom. "If pilots navigated the way [most] teachers teach," says Wiliam, now deputy director of the Institute of Education in London and former senior research director for the Educational Testing Service (ETS), "they would leave London, head west, and at the end of eight hours, ask, 'Is this New York?'"

Even teachers who check for students' understanding at the end of every lesson seldom get enough information to guide instruction, he adds. "They make up a question at the spur of the moment, ask the whole class, six kids raise their hands, and one answers," Wiliam says. "That's what I did as a teacher. But how dumb is that?"

"Teachers need better data to make instructional decisions," he adds.

THE USES OF BENCHMARK TESTING

Wiliam claims his research has been misinterpreted to suggest that *any* periodic assessment is an effective intervention. Jumping on the formative assessment bandwagon, test publishers have begun selling benchmark or early warning assessments linked to their end-of-year tests that indicate whether students are on track to pass. According to Tim Wiley, a senior analyst at Eduventures, LLC, these assessments represent the fastest-growing segment of the testing industry. Total spending on such instruments is approximately $150 million.

Stuart Kahl, president and CEO of Measured Progress, a testing firm based in Dover, N.H., cautions that benchmark tests are designed to obtain information about groups rather than individuals and should not be confused with formative assessment. The tests usually include only a handful of items on each topic in order to survey knowledge across an entire unit. But while one or two items can provide information on the skills of an entire class or a school, they do not yield enough information about an individual student's understanding to guide instructional decisions. For instance, if three quarters of the class miss both questions on multiplication, the teacher knows she needs to revisit this topic. But are these computational errors or conceptual problems? This kind of test is not likely to reveal the answer for any particular student.

Measured Progress produces a series of benchmark tests known as Progress Toward Standards. Kahl notes that these kinds of tests can be useful for interim program evaluation and for identifying patterns of performance. For example, if girls score better than boys across the board, that may spur schools to examine curriculum and instructional practices. But Kahl agrees with the University of Colorado's Shepard that the interim tests do not provide the type of information about individual student progress that appropriate formative assessments provide.

"Formative assessment is a range of activities at the classroom level [that] teachers use day in and day out to see if kids are getting it while they're teaching it," he says.

FORMATIVE ASSESSMENT TECHNIQUES
Districts and schools using formative assessments employ a variety of techniques. For instance, commercial companies are developing a variety of new assessment tools, ranging from handheld electronic "clickers" that allow students to register their responses to teachers' questions to instructional software programs that incorporate checks on student understanding. This helps teachers gauge the progress of the entire class, not just the students who raise their hands. Some six million students are using such programs at a cost of about $120 million, according to Eduventures' Wiley.

Some curriculum programs also include formative assessment techniques to help teachers gauge student understanding while they are teaching, notes Shepard. For example, a mathematics program might ask students to multiply 3 by 4 in three different ways: by making sets of three, by calculating the area of a floor, and by counting by fours. A right answer on any of these indicates that a student grasps the concept of multiplication. Otherwise, Shepard says, "you don't know if the student doesn't understand the concept or multiplication facts."

At ETS, Wiliam developed a series of workshops called Keeping Learning on Track to help teachers develop formative assessment strategies and monitor their own progress. These workshops have been conducted in 28 districts, including Cleveland. The workshops revolve around five key strategies: sharing expectations for learning, effective questioning, providing meaningful feedback, student self-assessment, and peer assessment among students. In each district, teachers come together every month to discuss how they implemented the strategies and the results they produced.

Donna Snodgrass, executive director for standards, curriculum, and classroom assessment for the Cleveland public school system, says the effort is essential because state tests provide too little information, and too late, to help teachers in the classroom. By the time the results come back, she notes, "kids are long gone, in another class."

"This gives them an idea of where kids are and what they can do about it," she says.

And it appears to be working. After two years, students' mathematics scores in the 10 participating Cleveland schools —among the lowest-performing in the city—rose four times faster than those in comparable schools. And while the program is aimed particularly at mathematics instruction, the program has also had an effect on reading achievement: Reading scores in the 10 schools increased four to five percentage points over two years. Snodgrass says these kinds of results have encouraged teachers to keep trying new strategies. The district is also planning to expand the program to additional schools.

INSIGHT INTO STUDENT MISTAKES

Other districts, like Boston, use more formal assessment instruments. FAST-R, which was developed by the Boston Plan for Excellence, uses 10 multiple-choice questions to probe student comprehension of a particular reading passage. The test can be used as a benchmark assessment, since it is aligned to state end-of-year tests, but it is also designed to help improve reading instruction, says Lisa Lineweaver, a senior program officer at the Boston Plan. It focuses in depth on only two skills (finding evidence and making inferences) and helps teachers diagnose reading difficulties on the basis of wrong answers. Answers are categorized as correct; "out of place," meaning that the answer is "a near miss" based on a misreading of the text; or "out of bounds," meaning that it is not based on the text. Comments on particular wrong answers can help teachers see where students are having trouble. Are they associating one word with another? "Plugging in" a plausible but irrelevant answer? Misapplying information gleaned elsewhere in the text?

The results come back a few days after the test is administered. After the assessment, the Boston Plan provides coaches who work with teachers to help them adjust instruction appropriately, based on student responses. Teachers are also encouraged to conference with children to probe more deeply into students' level of background knowledge and reasoning processes. "There is no way of knowing for sure what a kid is thinking unless you know the kid," Lineweaver says.

This chapter originally appeared in the November/December 2006 issue of the Harvard Education Letter.

FOR FURTHER INFORMATION

P. Black and D. Wiliam. "Assessment and Classroom Learning." *Assessment in Education* 5, no. 1 (1998): 7–74.

P. Black and D. Wiliam. "Inside the Black Box: Raising Standards through Classroom Assessment." *Phi Delta Kappan* 80, no. 2 (1998): 139–148. Available online at http://www.pdkintl.org/kappan/kbla9810.htm.

L. A. Shepard. "The Role of Classroom Assessment in Teaching and Learning." (CSE Technical Report 517.) Los Angeles: University of California, Los Angeles, Graduate School of Education and Information Studies, National Center on Evaluation, Standards, and Student Testing, 2000.

CHAPTER 8

Adding Value to Student Assessment

Does "value-added assessment" live up to its name?

by Anand Vaishnav

When English teacher Dawna Vanderpool returned to school last fall, she did what many teachers do: She pored over her eighth graders' test results from the previous year, searching for clues about how much they had learned and what aspects of her teaching had or had not been effective. Instead of relying on a single benchmark to measure achievement, however—for instance, whether a student scored as "proficient" on a statewide language arts test—Vanderpool measured each student's progress by comparing his or her actual test score to the score the student had been expected to receive, a prediction calculated on the basis of performance on annual tests in previous years.

Vanderpool's school, the DuBois Area Middle School in rural Pennsylvania, is one of a growing number of schools around the country that have implemented value-added assessment, which allows teachers and principals to evaluate not just the achievement of individual students, but how much "value" teachers add to student learning, taking into account how far behind or how far ahead students are academically before they enter a classroom.

The value-added pilot project in which Vanderpool's school is involved breaks data into quintiles according to students' achievement levels, to show the rate of progress each subgroup has made. To Vanderpool's surprise, she discovered that her lowest-achieving and highest-achieving students made more progress than expected, but her middle-achieving students fell short of predicted gains. Although their raw test scores were respectable, these students simply weren't learning as rapidly as their peers at either end of the spectrum.

The fact that she could see differences in the progress students were making at different levels prompted Vanderpool, now in her twelfth year of teaching, to reexamine her lessons. She realized she might have made too many assumptions about her average achievers—for example, that they already knew how to revise their essays without one-on-one assistance. The value-added results also led Vanderpool to wonder whether these students were well enough prepared to benefit from the group work she was assigning them. She now spends more time in full-class discussions. "I could see that making changes was necessary," she says.

GAINING GROUND

Since the early 1990s, when Tennessee began using value-added assessment statewide, the concept has picked up steam in big-city school systems like Dallas and Seattle, and in rural hamlets around the country. Large states such as Ohio and Pennsylvania have implemented value-added pilot projects at dozens of schools, and both will expand the method statewide in the next two to three years.

Education Week recently reported that at least 400 districts are using value-added analyses provided by the SAS Institute in North Carolina, a private firm at the forefront of the value-added movement. The firm's value-added assessment and research division is headed by William L. Sanders, a former University of Tennessee researcher whose design for the state of Tennessee has become the model for value-added assessment nationwide.

One factor contributing to the growing popularity of value-added assessment is the emphasis on accountability in the No Child Left Behind Act. The federal law requires that schools make "adequate yearly progress" (AYP) on test scores or face sanctions. Schools must raise test scores from one year to the next—even though the yearly comparisons measure different groups of children with varying educational needs. As a result, the fact that one year's fourth graders score higher than the previous year's may have more to do with cohort differences than with changes in instruction or learning.

Some observers say the value-added approach is preferable to the more traditional AYP model because it measures the same students over time. Schools with a majority of low-achieving students can get credit for boosting their performance beyond what might have been predicted for these children, even if the schools fall short of state benchmarks. Proponents also say that value-added assessment allows high-achieving schools with large numbers of advanced students to examine their stellar test scores and determine whether students are really being pushed to achieve at ever-higher levels or are merely coasting on past success.

The *Washington Post* reported that at least 16 state school superintendents have asked the U.S. Department of Education to permit them to use value-added assessment or similar methods in determining whether their schools are making adequate yearly progress. The government has yet to respond, but districts and states continue to experiment with value-added approaches.

"If it's done right, value-added assessment gives us a way of evaluating teachers and schools fairly," says David N. Plank, codirector of Michigan State University's Education Policy Center. "We know very well that poor kids, non-English-speaking kids, kids from racial minorities come to school often a year or two behind their middle-class white peers. To expect the school to instantaneously make up that deficit is simply unreasonable. And so what value-added assessment does is give us the possibility of identifying where kids are and how far they've come—which is the only fair standard against which to judge teachers and schools."

DRIVING SCHOOL CHANGE

Wickliffe Elementary School in Wickliffe, Ohio, a suburb of Cleveland, provides an example of how value-added assessment can work at the schoolwide level. The school, which includes students in prekindergarten through grade 4, tests students annually in the spring and sends the scores to the SAS Institute for analysis. Using a complicated formula that allows them to compare each student's current scores with his or her previous scores on other annual standardized tests, such as the Iowa Test of Basic Skills or statewide standards-based tests, researchers at the institute calculate how much progress the student made in the previous year and predict his or her progress for the coming year.

The school receives an analysis of its spring test results in the late summer or early fall. The data can then be grouped at the classroom, grade, or school level, as well as by performance level or other subcategories, so that school staff can see how well a student is progressing relative to his or her classmates; whether one class or school is progressing faster than another; or whether there are overall drops in performance from one grade to another—as children enter middle school or high school, for example.

Reviewing Wickliffe Elementary's value-added data, principal Karen Wolf discovered one year that her teachers were boosting the performance of their lower- and middle-performing fourth graders, but not their high achievers. Despite their high scores on measures of achievement, the value-added data suggested to Wolf that these students were capable of learning more. As a result, Wickliffe teachers added more enrichment activities to the curriculum, such as independent projects and tougher, more analytical tasks.

"[Value-added assessment] shows the mean student score and the mean predicted score, so you know if you're on target for achieving what you would hope to," Wolf says. "It allows you to see if you are hitting all of your ranges of students equally—and we weren't in every content area."

Another benefit of value-added assessment, Wolf says, is that it can provide encouragement to teachers who work with large numbers of low-performing students. At Wickliffe, as in other schools, these students often fall short of state and federal proficiency goals. But through the school's value-added assessment data, Wickliffe teachers were able to see that students were nonetheless progressing from the beginning of the year to the end. The school recently was named an Ohio Hall of Fame School for high achievement, and Wolf credits value-added assessment with helping to boost Wickliffe's results.

AN INEXACT SCIENCE

Despite good reviews from some educators, experts are split on whether value-added assessment lives up to its promises. Like all data analysis driven by standardized tests, value-added assessment has its limitations. First, it relies on narrow measures of what schools teach and what children learn. In addition, value-added assessment rests on predictions of how much academic ground students will gain in a given year—an inexact science at best. The statistical calculations involved are highly technical, and since the skills and content students are expected to master may vary substantially from year to year, predictions of progress can be difficult or even misleading. Controversy also rages over some of the conclusions schools draw from value-added assessments. Can teachers really be the sole source of all academic gains or losses? What about changes in family circumstances or other life events?

Another problem is in finding out exactly what teachers are doing to "add value"—and in figuring out how to transfer those strategies to other teachers who need help. Even in Tennessee, which implemented value-added assessment in the early 1990s, teachers have not used the system to its fullest, says Graham Greeson, manager of the research division for the 50,000-member Tennessee Education Association. The state is only now beginning to beef up its training for educators in using value-added data, Greeson says, although some districts have done the training on their own.

In addition, Tennessee is unusual in that officials there permit value-added assessment to be used in evaluating teachers—a politically tricky use of the data that Ohio and Pennsylvania have not touched. Michigan's law expressly forbids it. But Greeson notes that no teacher has been dismissed because he or she has poor value-added scores, and he doubts that principals are using value-added data in this way. The teacher "gain scores"—how a student grew under a particular teacher—go only to the teacher and the principal. "It's been out there, it's been reported in report cards, but people have been reluctant to really buy into it and use it [for teacher evaluation]," Greeson says.

The role of socioeconomic factors in value-added assessment is also in dispute. Student backgrounds continue to influence not just where students start but how rapidly they progress—how much value teachers add, in other words. Sanders's method does not account for differences in student background because individual students are compared only to themselves. But in Dallas, students' socioeconomic background is a part of the school system's value-added assessment. At the school level, for example, Dallas employs statistical techniques to control for factors such as student mobility and the number of students receiving free or reduced-price lunches. These factors, which Dallas administrators term "fairness variables," are taken into account in calculating each school's value-added results.

Joseph Martineau, a psychometrician for the Michigan Department of Education, has written an article soon to be published in the *Journal of Educational and Behavioral Statistics* in which he questions the validity of value-added assessment. Martineau argues that the huge differences in content that students need to learn from grade to grade make impossible the kind of performance predictions on which value-added assessment rests.

"In my opinion, it is not working at all the way people think it is working," Martineau says. "It doesn't make any sense to talk about growth or value added if you're not measuring the same thing at each time point. It's like measuring height in third grade, weight in fourth grade, trying to equate the scale, and subtracting them from each other."

Plank, of the Education Policy Center at Michigan State, puts it another way: "In third grade, you may have kids in a language arts assessment who are doing a lot of spelling, a lot of word recognition, a lot of basic vocabulary. In eighth grade, you expect kids to do interpretive reading, much more content, and much less basic skills. You can't compare a third-grade score to an eighth-grade score because they're measuring completely different things."

Still, Plank does not dismiss value-added assessment outright; he simply believes that not all of the necessary questions have yet been asked about this relatively young practice.

"The bottom line is simply to say there are significant technical problems that have to be addressed if we're going to make extensive use of value-added assessments in judging teachers and schools," notes Plank. "If you don't get the assessment system right, then you can end up making unfair judgments about teachers. You can give them credit for the work of teachers in previous years, or penalize them for the work of teachers in previous years. Technical problems become critically important if you're going to design a system that gives you accurate information about how teachers perform. But the logic of it, I think, is indisputable."

This chapter originally appeared in the May/June 2005 issue of the Harvard Education Letter.

FOR FURTHER INFORMATION

D. Ballou. "Sizing Up Test Scores." *Education Next* 2, no. 2 (Summer 2002): 10–15. Available online at www.educationnext.org/20022/10.html

J. Mahoney. "Why Add Value in Assessment?" *The School Administrator* (December 2004): 16–18. Available online at www.aasa.org/publications/sa/2004_12/mahoney_12.htm

D.F. McCaffrey, J.R. Lockwood, D.M. Koretz, and L.S. Hamilton. *Evaluating Value-Added Models for Teacher Accountability.* Santa Monica, CA: RAND Education, 2003. Available online at www.rand.org/pubs/monographs/2004/RAND_MG158.pdf

Pennsylvania Value-Added Assessment System. Available online at www.iu13.k12.pa.us/inst_init_vaas.shtml

Tennessee Value-Added Assessment System. Available online at www.state.tn.us/education/tstvaas.htm

CHAPTER 9

Performance vs. Attainment

The double standard for accountability in American high schools

By Richard F. Elmore

I t was a fairly standard high school visit. I met Kevin, the principal of Belle Glade High School, in his office at 7:15 A.M. and spent most of the day visiting classrooms.[1] Kevin is an experienced high school administrator in his second year at Belle Glade. Belle Glade enrolls students from a suburban community with one of the highest median family incomes in its region. The school is surrounded by well-appointed homes on multi-acre lots; its student parking lot is populated by late-model SUVs with roof racks and elliptical stickers with mysterious letters on them. More than 90 percent of the students at Belle Glade go on to college.

At the end of the day, I presented what has become a fairly standard set of observations:

- The typical teaching practice is a low-level form of the standard American IRE model—teacher (I)nitiates, student (R)esponds, teacher (E)valuates. Some students at Belle Glade call this the "What am I thinking?" game.

---

[1] Both Belle Glade and Kevin are pseudonyms.

- The general level of student affect toward learning is low, distant, unengaged.
- Despite the obvious homogeneity of the student body, the school is divided into four distinct academic tracks. The only obvious difference between them is the heavy volume of homework at the "honors" and "advanced" levels.
- There are significant variations in teachers' expectations from classroom to classroom. (However, no one could explain why, nor did anyone acknowledge the striking differences in skill and ability among teachers.)

My sense was that Belle Glade was cruising on its reputation and on the social capital of its community. When I said this to Kevin, the principal, he responded, "That's the world I live and work in every day—very mediocre teaching, very low-level work, mountains of mindless homework, and very flat student engagement and affect."

Kevin explained further: "The biggest problem for me is that everyone thinks this is a fabulous place because everyone gets into college (or at least we don't talk about the ones who don't). We look good on the state accountability test, although there are signs that we are not challenging at least a third of our students. But all the parents, the kids, and school board really care about is whether kids are getting into college. It's very hard to get leverage under these circumstances."

ADVANCING WITHOUT LEARNING

Belle Glade is an example of the most powerful accountability system at work in most American high schools—what I call the *attainment* system, designed to advance students smoothly through successive levels of schooling.

Most people equate accountability with federal- and state-mandated tests designed to measure students' *performance*—that is, their academic learning. Many states stipulate that students must score at a certain level on a statewide test in order to get a high school diploma; under the federal No Child Left Behind law, schools whose students perform poorly will also be subject to sanctions ranging from student transfers to closure and reconstitution.

In most of our schools, *attainment* and *performance* are only loosely related. That is, it is possible for students to advance from grade to grade, to accumulate the requisite credits in the requisite courses, to secure the necessary credentials for advancement to college, and finally to enroll in college, without meeting any specific standards of academic performance. Likewise, students who perform acceptably on standards-based tests may fail to negotiate the attainment structure, usually because they lack the social capital to make the necessary connections to higher education. It is not surprising that these are predominantly poor students and students of color.

Schools as privileged as Belle Glade operate in an environment in which, for all practical purposes, performance-based accountability doesn't exist, or exists only as a minor public relations problem. On average, Belle Glade students do well enough on state-mandated assessments that the tests don't represent any significant threat to either the school or its students. Attainment is the primary goal for Belle Glade's students and their families, and the one for which administrators are held most closely accountable. As a result, it is less important that the school provide high-quality learning for its students than that it (a) look like an attainment machine (hence the heavy-duty signaling to parents through the tracking system and the homework requirements for "higher-level" courses) and (b) provide a transcript that looks like one a college-bound student shou ld have. In fact, since attainment is largely a function of social class, most of these machinations are probably unnecessary. I have often thought that it would be an interesting social experiment to put all of the students entering schools like Belle Glade in cryogenic storage for four years, grant them diplomas at the end of that time, and then observe whether there were any discernible difference in their rates of college acceptance. My bet is that there would not be.

FAILURE DOWN THE ROAD

Schools that follow the attainment system may look like they are successful. But in many cases they are failing their students—and not only in the ways that are obvious from the story outlined above.

There are two systemic problems with the disconnect between performance and attainment in American high schools. First, the attainment system produces large numbers of students who are not ready for college work. About 70 percent of the nation's 2.5 million high school graduates go on to some form of postsecondary education within two years of graduation, and the vast majority of these students—about 70 percent—intend to complete college when they enroll. But about half of these high school graduates have to take remedial courses before they can begin the standard curriculum, and about 40 percent of those who earn more than ten college credits fail to complete a bachelor's degree. These disconnects between high school and college are present for some students in all high schools, including schools like Belle Glade, and they are chronic in many schools. For large numbers of students, the attainment system simply doesn't work.

Second, the performance-attainment disconnect establishes a double standard that severely disadvantages students in schools with high proportions of poor students and students of color. These schools have been told by the "official" accountability system that their job is to improve student performance, on the theory that students who learn at demonstrably higher levels will be more successful in later life. But as Kevin and other high school administrators in affluent communities know, the real rewards of education accrue to students who gain access to and finish college. Some principals of schools with high proportions of poor students and students of color have figured this out and have learned to connect students with college placement networks. But just as attainment does not equate to performance, successful performance does not necessarily lead to success in attainment, least of all for students with low social capital.

The performance-attainment dichotomy cannot be addressed without long-term, systemic change. But a few things could be done in the short term:

1. Eliminate—or at least ameliorate—the double standard that benefits one accountability system over the other. Specifically, no student should be deprived of a high school diploma on the basis of test scores alone. Similarly, standards applied to assess the quality of teaching and learning should be equally rigorous from school to school.
2. Make high schools accountable not just for college placement, but also for students' subsequent educational performance and attainment. Schools should be evaluated on measures such as the proportion of students requiring remediation in higher education and the baccalaureate success rate of students enrolling in college.
3. The academic work expected of high school students should be benchmarked against expectations for higher-level college work, not against teachers' subjective and individual assessments of students' capabilities.

Today's high schools are responding to mixed messages about accountability—are they responsible for improving performance or ensuring attainment? The stakes are high: to

pursue either goal at the expense of the other is to risk failing their students. Educators and policymakers need to ensure that schools are uniformly held accountable for both sets
of goals.

*This chapter originally appeared in the September/October 2004 issue of
the* Harvard Education Letter.

FOR FURTHER INFORMATION

C. Adelman. *Answers in the Tool Box: Academic Intensity, Attendance
Patterns, and Bachelor's Degree Attainment.* Washington, DC: U.S. Department of Education, Office of Educational Research and Improvement,
1999.

M. Kirst and K.R. Bracco. "Bridging the Great Divide: How the K–12
and Postsecondary Split Hurts Students, and What Can Be Done About
It." In M. Kirst and A. Venezia. *From High School to College: Improving
Opportunities in Postsecondary Education.* San Francisco: Jossey-Bass,
2004.

B. Schneider. "Strategies for Success: High School and Beyond." In D.
Ravitch, ed., *Brookings Papers on Educational Policy.* Washington, DC:
Brookings Institution, 2003.

PART III

Diversity and Achievement

CHAPTER 10

Recent Research on the Achievement Gap

Ronald Ferguson discusses how lifestyle factors and classroom culture affect black-white differences

For more than a decade, economist Ronald Ferguson has studied achievement gaps. In 2002, he created the Tripod Project for School Improvement, a professional development initiative that uses student and teacher surveys to measure classroom conditions and student engagement by race and gender. The findings inform strategies to raise achievement and narrow achievement gaps. A senior research associate at Harvard's Kennedy School of Government, Ferguson is director and faculty cochair of the Achievement Gap Initiative at Harvard University. He spoke with the Harvard Education Letter *about the most recent findings from the Tripod Project surveys.*

How do you define "achievement gap"?

There are a lot of different achievement gaps. The achievement gap that I focus the most on is the gap between students of different racial groups whose parents have roughly the same amount of education. It concerns me that black kids whose parents have college degrees on average have much lower test scores than white kids whose parents have college degrees, for example. You can take just about any level of parental education and we have these big gaps.

How much progress has been made in closing black-white achievement gaps?

Huge progress since 1970, not much progress since 1990. Sixty-two percent of the overall black-white reading-score gap for 17-year-olds disappeared between 1971 and 1988. About one-third of the math-score gap disappeared during the same period. Over the last several years the gap has narrowed significantly for both 9- and 13-year-olds, but there's been a bit of backsliding for the older teens.

There's been enough progress to establish firmly that these gaps are not written in stone. Even IQ gaps are narrowing. Measurements of the intelligence of kids less than one year old show virtually no racial or social-class differences, yet racial and social-class achievement gaps are firmly established by the time students start kindergarten. Something happens before kindergarten that produces differences in proficiency.

Achievement gaps are not facts of nature. They are mostly because of differences in life experience. We've got to figure out how to get all kids the kinds of experiences that really maximize access to middle-class skills. That's the challenge.

Some say that social inequities must be solved before we can close achievement gaps; others say it's the schools' responsibility to close them. Where do you stand?

First of all, it's not an either/or question. If you are talking about having black achievement levels and white achievement levels that are completely the same, then yeah, you have to deal with quite a few challenges in the domain of wealth and social capital, but that's in the long run. In the near term, I think we can make substantial progress by affecting home intellectual climate and lifestyle as they affect achievement. The big idea that frames my thinking these days is lifestyle. Even in school, the notion is to try to provoke lifestyle changes that cause people to be a bit more focused on cultivating a love of learning among kids.

Isn't talking about lifestyle factors a way of blaming the victim?

Your motivation can be to explain why we have achievement gaps or it can be to seek levers to pull in order to reduce achievement gaps. I'm seeking levers to pull in order to reduce the gaps. I don't care whose fault it is, really. If it's the case that reading scores could rise if parents pushed their kids to do more leisure reading at home or took the television out of the bedroom, why not do it? Or why not at least tell parents that that's an option that they have? I think most parents would want to know.

Still, virtually every school can make progress even if the family achieves zero change. They'll do better if parents do more, but no school, no institution, none of us is as good as we can be. Pretty much every school has a way to improve. I've been working in schools for almost a decade, paying a lot of attention to teacher-student relationships and some of the ways that teachers understand or misunderstand kids. There's a spiral of mutual causation that can lead classrooms to be either terrible places or really nice places. A lot of it you can characterize as lifestyle.

How does your research help schools change their lifestyles to support achievement?

The project that I run is called the Tripod Project because we address three pieces: content, pedagogy, and relationships. And what vexes me most in the schools that I work with is that it's so hard to get people to spend time studying the work of the students who don't do very well. Because if our main concern is material on which students don't do well, then why don't we look at where the breakdown is and work on that? Just take the assignments of the students who have done poorly, sit down together, and figure out what it is that they didn't know; why we think they didn't know it; and talk about how to alter instructional approaches to help them.

We use a protocol called Teaching the Hard Stuff to talk about whether success was feasible for the student, whether the kids were focused or not, and why they may not have been focused. People like the protocol, they enjoy using it, and they almost always get up from the table with new insights, but they don't set aside more time to do it more frequently.

What does Teaching the Hard Stuff involve and what do teachers learn?

It's an hour-long protocol for looking at student work. Teachers discover all kinds of things. At least half the time the problem is with the way the assignment was written: The assignment wasn't really testing what the teacher was trying to test; or there was a vocabulary word that had two meanings; or the context for the problem was a context the students weren't familiar with and so the student couldn't solve the problem. If the achievement gap is based on the nature of the experiences that students have, and if schools don't scaffold appropriately on the understandings that kids bring from their different experiences, then kids can't construct the new understandings.

One of my favorite examples is a Pythagorean theorem problem: How far does a catcher need to throw the ball in order to throw out a runner who is trying to steal second base if the bases are 90 feet apart? If kids don't know there's a right angle at first base, they can't solve that question.

Where schools may contribute to the achievement gap is by not scaffolding appropriately for different kids, not differentiating instruction in ways that are grounded in what kids actually bring to the classroom. Teachers try to make work interesting and relevant by using real-world examples. But which real-world example will your kids understand? And if they don't understand it, will they admit it? In our surveys we find that black kids in particular are concerned all the way through school with whether people think they are smart or not. If you are concerned with whether you think people think you're smart, you are not going to speak up and show your ignorance as often. So if what the teacher just said doesn't make sense to you—particularly if you are in a racially integrated classroom and you think the other kids are ahead of you—you are more likely to misbehave and pretend like you weren't trying anyway, because it's better to look lazy than stupid.

What other misperceptions does your research point to?

There are sometimes misperceptions about how much parents care. In our surveys, the higher the percentage of black kids in the classroom, the lower the teacher's estimate of how many kids will say that their parents asked them what they learned in school that day. When we ask kids the same question, we don't pick up racial differences.

Now you *do* pick up racial differences when you get at parenting practices more directly: TVs in the bedroom, which our studies show are associated with sleepiness in class; whether kids say they watch TV at home more than anything else; how much leisure reading they do; how many books are provided in the house. Eighty percent of black kids in our surveys at the elementary level have TVs in their bedroom. Much smaller percentages of white kids do.

Another misperception that folks often have is that kids who misbehave don't want to learn. Teachers see that black kids misbehave on average more than white kids do. There's not much dispute about that—the kids self-report worse behavior. Also, black kids have lower homework completion rates than white kids do, which they also self-report. So what do you infer? You say, well, they don't care as much and they aren't trying too hard.

In my surveys, I find that even though black students self-report more misbehavior and less homework completion, they also self-report spending almost exactly the same amount of time on homework as their white classmates. They also self-report equal or higher endorsement of the statement "My friends think it's important to work hard to get high grades in school." They are motivated, but there's some subtlety to it, because they have conflicting motivations, conflicting pressures. Sometimes they're just trying to fit in with friends, to be liked inside a culture of behavior that no one student created and no one student can single-handedly reform. They are part of a peer culture where certain patterns of behavior do have oppositional elements, but they are not opposition to high achievement. Paradoxically, their assertiveness is a quest for respect: It shows opposition to the kinds of subordination and toleration of disrespect that blacks have had to put up with over centuries. Kids are saying, "We're not taking that. . . . You can't face me down in front of one of my friends and yell at me or fuss at me and have me not say something back to you."

This seems to challenge the "acting white" hypothesis—that black kids are afraid to achieve because high achievement is seen as acting white.

Based on the survey results that I get back from students, I believe it's a misperception that kids think getting high grades is acting white. It's really a matter of personal style. Students who get high grades will often have personal styles that seem to violate the endorsed expressions of racial authenticity: they may speak proper English too much in informal settings; they may listen to rock music instead of rap; they may be a little too happy-go-lucky in their attitudes. In order to fit in with your friends, you don't have to be a low achiever or resist high grades, but you do need to be able to speak in informal settings the way kids speak in informal settings, you do have to be the kind of kid who doesn't tolerate disrespect without a response even if it comes from an adult in an authority position. Among black kids, self-esteem rises as grades rise all the way through an A, *except* if it's the kid who doesn't fit in socially, in which case—if it's a male—self-esteem drops as they move from a B to an A average. This is not true for white kids.

How do these findings relate to your research on teasing?

Some of the peer dynamics around achievement, such as teasing each other for making mistakes, may not be visible to teachers, but they are problems as early as first grade. In first-grade classes where fewer than 25 percent of the students are white or Asian, I find that more than half agree that classmates tease other kids for making mistakes. Teasing for making mistakes in majority white and Asian classes is about 20 percentage points lower. Kids who worry that other classmates tease kids for making mistakes report that they worry more that they may not measure up to their classmates. Worry is anxiety, and anxiety interferes with concentration.

What can teachers do to foster student engagement and create a positive peer culture?

I have data at the elementary level that show that if kids don't think the teacher both loves to help them and holds them to a high standard—what I call a "high help/high perfectionism" classroom—their behavior can deteriorate and their engagement can deteriorate, and the teachers are more likely to think that the kids just don't want to learn. If the class is less than 25 percent white or Asian and the students rate the teacher as offering both low help and low perfectionism, kids can treat each other pretty poorly. All you need is about a quarter of the kids in the class who don't think their questions are welcome to get a pretty uncollegial classroom environment. The challenge to the teacher is being able to signal, "I love to help you" *and* "We're never fully satisfied until we can do it correctly." When working with kids who come from difficult backgrounds, and who don't bring a whole lot for you to scaffold on some of the time, you've really got to understand these kids. You've got to understand what they don't understand and what their misunderstandings are, and you've got to have the confidence to say, "If these children tell me what they are thinking, I can clear up any confusions that they have, and at the end of the day they're going to understand what I am trying to teach them."

Over 80 percent of kids in any classroom say they plan to do their best all year long, if you ask them in the fall. The only ones that are still near that level in the spring—if the vast majority are nonwhite and non-Asian—are kids in high help/high perfectionism classrooms. We need to give teachers the learning experiences that help them reach and teach some of the kids who they are struggling to understand if we want kids to persist and do their best work all year.

This chapter originally appeared in the November/December 2006 issue of the Harvard Education Letter.

FOR FURTHER INFORMATION

J.B. Diamond. "Are We Barking Up the Wrong Tree? Rethinking Oppositional Culture Explanations for the Black/White Achievement Gap." Available online at http://agi.harvard.edu/events.Papers.php

W.T. Dickens and J.R. Flynn. "Black Americans Reduce the Racial IQ Gap: Evidence from Standardization Samples." Available online at http://agi.harvard.edu/events.Papers.php

R. Ferguson. *What Doesn't Meet the Eye: Understanding and Addressing Racial Disparities in High-Achieving Suburban Schools.* Oakbrook, IL: North Central Regional Educational Laboratory, 2002. Available online at http://www.ksg.harvard.edu/tripodproject/about.html#whatis

R.G. Fryer Jr. and S.D. Levitt. "Testing for Racial Differences in the Mental Ability of Young Children." Available online at http://agi.harvard.edu/events.Papers.php

The Tripod Project. www.ksg.harvard.edu/tripodproject/

CHAPTER 11

Making Schools Safer for LGBT Youth

Despite signs of progress, harassment persists

by Michael Sadowski

S helby is an openly gay junior at a large suburban high school near Boston.[1] On most days, she says, she feels lucky to attend a relatively affluent, liberal school that offers her "an excellent education, opportunities to pursue my passions, and a fairly safe place for me to express my sexual orientation." Issues like same-sex marriage, now legal in Massachusetts, have been discussed in several of her classes, and incidents of homophobia are addressed swiftly.

Nonetheless, Shelby says the undercurrents of homophobia run deep among her peers. Students are quick to use expressions like "That's so gay!" or to hurl antigay slurs against opponents at sporting events. Despite its policies and its reputation, she says, her school sometimes seems like an unsafe place to be a lesbian, gay, bisexual, or transgender (LGBT) student.[2]

---

[1] Student names used in this article are pseudonyms.

[2] Language is a problematic issue when writing about this group of young people. I use the abbreviation "LGBT" and the term "sexual minority

"Our school promotes safety, diversity, and tolerance as part of its mission, but does the message get across?" she asks. "From the way students act, it seems that the answer is largely no."

Dena attends a much smaller high school in a more conservative town than Shelby's, about 60 miles away, where she has come out as bisexual. "I hear derogatory comments such as 'gay,' 'queer,' or 'fag' at least ten times daily," she reports. "My school doesn't have many openly queer students, and those who do have the courage to be open about their sexuality are ridiculed, harassed, and assaulted." Last year, for example, a group of girls on a school bus put gum in Dena's hair and called her names like "dyke," "lesbian," and "bitch." Although the school has a "no tolerance" harassment policy, Dena says school administrators simply told the offending girls that their behavior was "inappropriate."

"The administrations in our schools . . . are in denial about how bad the harassment really is," she says.

YOUTH CULTURE: "GAY-BLIND"?

The experiences reported by Dena and Shelby run counter to some recent reports that suggest today's teenagers—growing up in an era of same-sex marriages and films like *Brokeback Mountain*—are much more accepting of their LGBT peers than their counterparts twenty, ten, or even five years ago.

Last summer, Ritch Savin-Williams, professor and chair of human development at Cornell University, raised eyebrows with the publication of his latest book, *The New Gay Teenager*, which was featured in an October 2005 *Time* magazine cover story on gay teens. In the book, Savin-Williams criti-

---

youth" to discuss this group of students as a whole, while recognizing that these terms actually encompass subgroups of adolescents who face both distinct and common issues in schools.

cizes much of the research on gay youth, charging that it has perpetuated a "suffering suicidal script" about these young people, the vast majority of whom are, by his account, "adapting quite well, thank you."

"The culture of contemporary teenagers easily incorporates its homoerotic members," he writes. "It's more than being gay-friendly. It's being gay-blind."

In addition to surveys and interviews he has been conducting since 1983, Savin-Williams points to the latest Hamilton College Hot Button Issues poll, a survey of 1,000 high school seniors conducted in November 2005 by the college and Zogby International, for evidence of this shift in youth values. The poll found that large majorities of high school seniors nationwide favor either legal marriage or civil unions for same-sex couples; adoption by same-sex couples; and laws banning job discrimination on the basis of sexual orientation.

"These kids have come so much further than adults have, or even their brothers and sisters in college," Savin-Williams says.

Savin-Williams cites the proliferation of gay-straight alliances (GSAs) as further evidence of changing school climates. GSAs are in-school groups formed by LGBT students and their "straight allies" to discuss homophobia, plan school events to raise awareness of LGBT issues, or simply hang out in a safe place. The number of GSAs has quadrupled in U.S. high schools since 2000. "While not long ago this issue was kept out of just about every school in the country, there are now more than 3,000 gay-straight alliances," Savin-Williams says. "Clearly, schools have accepted or at least tolerated these organizations."

ATTITUDES VS. ACTIONS

If attitudes among students and school administrators have changed so dramatically, why do students like Shelby and

Dena—who attend school in one of the most LGBT-supportive areas of the country—still feel so unsafe?

"The problem of harassment in schools has not gone away," says Kevin Jennings, a former classroom teacher and executive director of the Gay, Lesbian & Straight Education Network (GLSEN), a New York–based organization dedicated to improving school climates for LGBT students. GLSEN's National School Climate Surveys, polls of LGBT students conducted every two years, have consistently found high levels of anti-LGBT harassment in schools across the country. Last year GLSEN also commissioned a national survey by the research firm Harris Interactive, which indicated that LGBT students face significant obstacles that prevent them from feeling safe and able to concentrate on learning in school.

Jennings is quick to point out that these surveys are not being used to portray LGBT students in a negative light; rather, they are intended to draw attention to the deficiencies of schools and other institutions in serving these young people effectively. "I don't think what we're doing is pathologizing the kids. We're not—the kids are great," Jennings says. "If we're pathologizing anything, it's the schools that don't do the right thing."

THE "LGBT-FRIENDLY" SCHOOL

To ensure that LGBT young people attend school in a safe environment that is conducive to learning, Jennings and others say, the first basic step is the establishment of a school policy explicitly stating that all students have the right to attend school free from harassment and discrimination. Beth Reis, a researcher and cochair of the Safe Schools Coalition, a Seattle-based organization that works with school districts to establish and enforce safe schools policies, says there are several characteristics that make up the "ideal" district antiharassment/antidiscrimination policy. First, she says, it must specifically cite the kinds of harassment and discrimination that are prohibited in school, explicitly mentioning such issues as race, gender, religion, sexual orientation, and gender expression as well as the kinds of language and behavior the policy covers. Second, she says, the policy must be accessible to students at all grade levels, since harassment and discrimination can and do take place from elementary through high school.

Other characteristics of effective school policies, Reis notes, include a comprehensive plan for dissemination; procedures for reporting any problems that arise; and an "anonymous option" that allows students to cite violations of the policy without identifying themselves, if doing so might place them at psychological or physical risk.

Still, as Shelby's and Dena's experiences attest, policies are only the beginning. Though research in this field is relatively new, a number of studies point to other elements that can contribute to the creation of an "LGBT-friendly" school:

Gay-straight alliances. A 2001 study of 1,646 students and 683 staff members from randomly selected schools, commissioned by the Massachusetts Department of Education and led by researcher Laura Szalacha, found that LGBT students in schools with GSAs were three times as likely to feel safe being out at school and were significantly less likely to hear homophobic slurs on a daily basis, compared to students in schools without GSAs. Numerous interview studies have further documented the power of GSAs in helping LGBT youth feel safe and supported at school.

Supportive teachers and faculty training. The Massachusetts Youth Risk Behavior Survey, which samples more than 3,000 students from randomly selected high schools every two years, has found that students are less likely to report feelings of depression or to attempt suicide if they feel that they have adults at school that they can talk to about things that are important to them. This finding is especially significant given the dramatically higher rates of suicidal behaviors among sexual minority youth. Szalacha's study found that in schools where faculty had been trained in LGBT youth issues, more than half of LGBT students said they felt they had the support of school faculty, compared to only about a quarter of LGBT students in schools where such trainings had not taken place.

Addressing the needs of LGBT youth of color. GLSEN's school climate surveys have found that LGBT students of color often face different forms of harassment and discrimination than their white LGBT peers. In the most recent poll, the vast majority of these young people (85 percent) said they had been harassed at school, and about half said they had experienced harassment based on both their race and their sexual orientation. Qualitative researchers like Lance McCready of Carleton College in Northfield, Minn., have found that the LGBT youth of color sometimes feel marginalized both by their peers of color and by other LGBT youth at school, and thus avoid groups like GSAs that might provide them with support. Experts say it is crucial to ensure that LGBT programs meet the needs of students of color as well as white students.

Understanding transgender issues. Issues affecting transgender students are widely considered to be the last frontier in efforts to ensure safer schools for sexual minority students. School faculty and staff often know the least about transgender students, or even what the word "transgender" means, Jennings notes. (In addition to transsexuals, transgender students include those who do not conform to traditional gender roles, such as dressing in ways that run contrary to gender norms.) Like LGBT youth of color, transgender youth face unique risks in school settings, according to the GLSEN school climate surveys. "Even within the category of LGBT students, the surveys have shown that transgender students have it worse than LGB kids, I think because gender difference is more visible," Jennings says. He stresses that training on LGBT issues must include specific discussion of how schools and classrooms can be made safer for transgender students.

BEYOND PROGRAMS AND POLICIES

Policies and programs aside, the quality of school life for LGBT students like Shelby and Dena seems to hinge most on the daily interactions between students and teachers—and, perhaps more important, among students themselves. The most critical step toward creating the "LGBT-friendly school" may therefore be to do what schools are charged to do in the first place: educate students. According to Reis, this education can take a number of forms, from displaying LGBT-related images throughout the school building to curriculum that acknowledges the contributions, the voices, and the history of LGBT people—not just on a special "gay day," but within the fabric of regular school subjects. Reis recommends reaching out to parents and community members in planning these kinds of efforts even in the face of resistance, since the alternative— neglecting LGBT education for fear of "making waves"—can have devastating consequences.

"I often tell people [who challenge the inclusion of LGBT issues in the curriculum] that in the 13 years they went to school, I doubt that the two young men who killed Matthew Shepard ever heard a teacher say anything positive or even neutral about gay, lesbian, bisexual, or transgender people," Reis says. "If they had, I wonder if he would be alive today."

This chapter originally appeared in the May/June 2006 issue of the Harvard Education Letter.

FOR FURTHER INFORMATION

Gay, Lesbian & Straight Education Network, 90 Broad St. 2nd Fl., New York, NY 10004; tel: (212) 727-0135. www.glsen.org

L. McCready. "When Fitting in Isn't an Option, or, Why Black Queer Males at a California High School Stay Away from Project 10." In K. K. Kumashiro, *Troubling Intersections of Race and Sexuality: Queer Students of Color and Anti-Oppressive Education*. Lanham, MD: Rowman & Littlefield, 2001.

Safe Schools Coalition, 10501 Meridian Ave. N., Seattle, WA 98133; tel: (206) 632–0662. www.safeschoolscoalition.org

R.C. Savin-Williams. *The New Gay Teenager*. Cambridge, MA: Harvard University Press, 2005.

L.A. Szalacha. "Safer Sexual Diversity Climates: Lessons Learned from an Evaluation of Massachusetts' Safe Schools Program for Gay and Lesbian Students." *American Journal of Education* 110, no. 1 (2003): 58–89.

CHAPTER 12

Eliminating Ableism

Thomas Hehir on the aims of special education

Thomas Hehir is professor of practice and director of the School Leadership Program at the Harvard Graduate School of Education and former director of the U.S. Department of Education's Office of Special Education Programs. In his new book, New Directions in Special Education, *Hehir addresses the challenges of eliminating ableism in schools.*

What do you mean by the term "ableism"?

Ableism is essentially like racism and sexism and homophobia. It's societal prejudice against people with disabilities, some of which is blatant—like when disabled people aren't able to attend an event because they use a wheelchair—and some of which is more subtle, such as the desire for disabled people to perform life tasks in the same ways as nondisabled people. In educational practice, this would be reflected in the desire for children with very little vision to read print as opposed to Braille; having deaf children read lips as opposed to signing; or having kids with physical disabilities spend an inordinate amount of time taking physical therapy so that they might walk—even if it's just a few stumbling steps—at the expense of taking academic instruction.

How do attitudes toward disability shape the goals of special education?

Special education is adrift as a field. People are often confused about what the goals of special education should be. When I do workshops with special ed directors, and I ask what the goal of special education should be, I get 20 different responses from 20 different people. Which is unfortunate, because if you're running a program, you should know where it's going!

Special education is so individualized that people often lack the bigger picture of what we should be accomplishing for all children with disabilities. I believe that what we should be doing in special education is *minimizing the impact* of disability and *maximizing the opportunity* to participate in the world. All our interventions should be directed toward that goal.

One issue you emphasize in your book is the importance of accommodations, such as the use of taped books or digitized text. How is that different from making modifications to the curriculum?

Teachers often speak of accommodations and modifications as if they are synonymous, when they are not. Accommodations are often needed for children with disabilities. They offer children access to the curriculum but do not change the content that is taught to the child, whereas modification often changes the content. People are very quick to modify curriculum for children with disabilities, which reflects, in my view, an assumption that these kids aren't capable.

It's not that modifications aren't appropriate under some circumstances. For instance, many children with mental retardation are not going to be on grade level in academic subjects. That doesn't mean that they can't profit from that subject, but it may have to be modified to the child's level. For kids with learning disabilities, modification can be appropriate in reading instruction or spelling—things that are directly related to their disability—but not in other areas.

An example of inappropriate modification would be a child with a learning disability who is required to do fewer math problems for homework because he reads slowly, as opposed to giving him a taped version of the assignment and expecting him to do what any other child does.

When is it appropriate to include children with disabilities in classes with nondisabled children and when is it appropriate to pull them out?

Some activists who are seeking to improve the world for people with disabilities have viewed inclusion as a vehicle with which to do that. They feel that children who are educated with disabled kids are likely to grow up more accepting of disability, and there is some research that shows that that may actually be the case.

But some people who are very dogmatic about inclusive education don't recognize the benefit of removal for certain kids. Sometimes being educated in the regular class doesn't minimize the impact of disability. For instance, years ago I taught kids with severe learning disabilities at the high school level who were virtual nonreaders. I did not integrate these kids into general education English classes because they needed very intensive work in reading. Placing them in that environment would not have provided the opportunities for them to learn to read.

You have said that sometimes, with individualized education programs (IEPs), "more is less." Can you say more about that?

If your goal is to minimize disability and maximize children's ability to participate, you want to have a lot of focus in an IEP. That's the only way you're going to have real change and real opportunity. Let's say you have an eighth grader who is dyslexic and is reading at a fourth-grade level, but at a rate that is one-third the rate of a typical reader. If you're going to minimize the impact of his disability, you need intensive intervention around reading, and probably writing and spelling as well. But you also need to problem-solve around how that child is going to access science, social studies, or great books. Reading is a gateway skill, and what we find in many dyslexic kids is that their disability begins to have a cumulative effect on their achievement in other areas.

I see a lot of IEPs for these kinds of kids where they're modifying the rest of the curriculum. You'll see all kinds of goals in science and in math. These IEPs can go on forever! And what they're going on forever about is dumbing down the curriculum. That's a disservice. A better plan would be to give the kid specialized reading intervention and to make sure he has access to digitized text in the rest of his subjects, so that he's learning at grade level.

What do you see as the potential benefits of standards-based education for children with special needs, and what do you see as the potential pitfalls?

Broadly speaking, I am a supporter of standards-based education because it forces people to confront the greatest ableist assumption in education, which is that kids with disabilities are incapable of achieving at a high level. The disability community has generally been supportive of standards-based reform for that reason.

But there are potential downsides here. Number one is high stakes. I think you have to differentiate between holding schools accountable for achieving high standards and holding kids accountable. If kids haven't been given opportunities to learn, that can be inappropriate. There's also the question of whether the accommodations in test-taking are robust enough for children with disabilities. So it's a complex issue.

FIRST PERSON SINGULAR

Narrative accounts by adults with disabilities can help educators understand the impact of social attitudes toward disability. Classic sources include:

Dianne L. Ferguson and Adrienne Asch, "Lessons from Life: Personal and Parental Perspectives on School, Childhood, and Disability," in *Schooling and Disability: Eighty-Eighth Yearbook of the National Society for the Study of Education: Part II*, ed. D. Biklen, D. Ferguson, and A. Ford. Chicago: University of Chicago Press, 1989.

Penny Ford, "Something to Be Gained: A Family's Long Road to Inclusive Schooling," in *Inclusion: Moving Beyond Our Fears*, ed. J. Rogers. Bloomington, IN: Phi Delta Kappa Center for Evaluation, Development, and Research, 1993.

Harlyn Rousso, "Fostering Healthy Self-Esteem, Part 1," in *Exceptional Parent* 14, no. 8 (1984).

Gregory Smith, "Backtalk: The Brother in the Wheelchair," in *Essence*, July 20, 2001.

What can schools do to create a more inclusive environment that does not reinforce ableism?

Generally speaking, the school should be accepting of the disabled children who would normally come to that school. Demographically, maybe 10 or 12 percent of kids will have disabilities. The vast majority of them will fall into four categories: learning disabilities, speech and language disorders, ADHD, and moderate behavioral and intellectual disabilities. That accounts for about 90 percent of the disability population.

So if you're going to be an inclusive school, you have to look at two key areas: reading and behavior. You will need a more diversified approach to the reading program. Similarly, you should develop positive, consistent strategies for dealing with behavior and discipline. If from the beginning you are developing consistent approaches to behavior and interventions for all kids, not just for disabled kids, you're going to be able to serve disabled kids better.

You should also consider as a faculty how you are going to make decisions around curricular accommodations and modifications. For instance, if primary-grade teachers make the decision to modify curriculum, it's going to have a cumulative effect: those kids might not be able to pass a high school exit exam.

One thing that has emerged from the literature on inclusion is that in order to do inclusive education correctly, you have to deal with the issue of teacher isolation. Decisions around behavior, around reading, around curriculum accommodations and modifications, need to be made consistently across the grades.

This chapter originally appeared in the January/February 2006 issue of the Harvard Education Letter.

CHAPTER 13

Finding High-Achieving Schools in Unexpected Places

Karin Chenoweth discusses what these successful schools have in common

In 2004, Karin Chenoweth, a longtime education writer and former Washington Post *columnist, took on a challenging assignment: find and write about neighborhood public schools that "demonstrate that all children can learn." Working with the Achievement Alliance and using a strict set of criteria, Chenoweth identified 15 schools and spent two years writing about them for a book,* "It's Being Done": Academic Success in Unexpected Schools, *recently published by Harvard Education Press. She spoke with the* Harvard Education Letter *about what she found in these schools, what they have in common, and why they are succeeding.*

Describe an "It's Being Done" school.

It's a high-achieving or rapidly improving school that has a substantial number of children of color or children of poverty, or both. In most cases, more than 90 percent of these students are scoring proficient or above on state tests, sometimes less if they are in states with higher standards. The schools profiled in the book include a mix of big and small, urban and suburban, and racially isolated and integrated schools. The criteria

I used are so stringent that it is safe to say that schools that meet all requirements are rare (see "'It's Being Done' School Criteria," p. 107). I consider such schools to be precious resources that need careful study.

What was it like to do all these school visits?

It was great. As a reporter, I've been in many schools, and for the most part they give me a headache. Schools can be so boring. I've been in schools that do things like make kids practice sitting for assemblies. Nobody practices how to sit in these schools. Kids were learning things all the time. These are really exciting places where people are very excited about what they do. They really renewed my faith in public education.

What distinguishes the schools in your book from run-of-the-mill schools or from "crummy poor-kid schools," as you call them?

Their relentless focus on instruction. That's what they talk about: What they need to teach and how to teach it. That's the main conversation in the schools. In crummy poor-kid schools, the conversation is dominated by "If we had better kids we would have a better school." I've heard versions of that I don't know how many times. Run-of-the-mill schools just teach to the high-achieving kids. That's the standard way schools are run. The rest of the students they just give assignments to, a lot of worksheets and such. Those schools may have some good teachers, but you can't count on the school to pick up on weak teaching.

What other important things do these high-achieving schools have in common?

For the most part, the principals distribute leadership very consciously, very deliberately. Teachers make very important decisions about finances, such as how to use Title I money; about operations, such as opening and dismissal; and about

"IT'S BEING DONE" SCHOOL CRITERIA

1. Significant population of children living in poverty and/or a significant population of children of color
2. Proficiency rates above 80 percent, or a very rapid improvement trajectory
3. Smaller achievement gaps than the state
4. Two years' worth of comparable data
5. High graduation rates and high proportion of freshmen who are seniors four years later (Promoting Power Index)
6. Annual Yearly Progress met
7. Open enrollment for neighborhood children (no magnet, charter, or exam schools)

curriculum and lesson plans. The principals really make the teachers part of running the school.

They also set up the school so teachers are successful. These schools are not easy places to be successful. When 90 percent of your students qualify for free or reduced-price lunch, they come with additional problems that many teachers feel very deeply about. So every aspect of the school day and school practice comes under scrutiny to ensure that there is no wasted time or effort.

The principals in rapidly improving schools are very smart. They celebrate every success and find everything they can to celebrate. They'll say, "We may not have gotten there this year, but look at this. We improved on this measure, and we're really going to improve next year on this other measure." Teachers feel supported.

Teachers *want* to work hard for these principals because they know they have their back. I've been in schools where if a teacher admits they're having trouble, the principal will say, "Well, if you're having trouble with that, that will be reflected in your evaluation." That would never happen in these schools. The principal would say something like, "You know who's really good at that? So-and-so. We'll get you in that classroom so you can observe."

Test scores were a big part of your criteria for choosing these schools, but you say they are not "drill-and-kill" schools. What role does test prep play in these schools?

It varies a little bit. They all make sure that the kids are not surprised by the test format. They do what some of them call "test sophistication"—"This is how a multiple-choice test is set up, how the answers are formulated." Some of them give practice tests, but they are all very conscious about not overdoing it.

Attitude also plays a big role in these profiles. Why?

If you think that nothing you do can make a difference for poor students or students of color, it saps your energy to do anything. Teachers have been told for years that there is nothing you can do to change demographic realities. Convincing teachers that they can have an effect, that they are important levers in children's learning—that's key to changing the way schools operate. If you can do something, that's an encouragement to try. If you can't, then you might as well worry about how long your lunch break is. There are really some teachers who cannot be convinced that they can or should try to teach poor children and children of color. They should not be in school.

Many of the schools in your book are led by wise, even charismatic, principals—to the point where you worried about what would happen to their schools when they retired. Isn't this a big problem in education reform?

I think a weak principal corps is a big problem. There's not enough good training on how to be a good principal. These principals in "It's Being Done" schools are very aware of the problems involved in replacing themselves, and it's one of the reasons they are very careful to distribute leadership in the school. They've spent a lot of time helping their teachers become as skilled as possible, so they know how to read data, for instance. It's not just the principal who understands how to do it. Some are very adamant that the teachers fill in the student data sheets themselves for this reason.

At bottom, a school has to have a good principal, but it doesn't necessarily have to have a brilliant principal. A good school leader sets the goals and helps the staff understand and meet the goals. That takes skill and knowledge, not necessarily charisma.

What did you learn from this project? What surprised you the most?

I had been worried that teachers and principals would really be burnt out by all the expectations placed on them. For the most part, that's not what I found. I found very energetic professionals who love their jobs. They did not set out to make good places to work but good places for the kids to learn. It turns out that those two things are not incompatible, and that was a nice surprise.

Are there some factors that people believe are important to turning around schools that really aren't?

I think some of the structural reforms that people focus on are not all that important. For example, the grade configurations of schools. Whether a school is K–8 or broken up into elementary and middle school is not as important as making sure that teachers know what needs to be taught at each grade level. Similarly, whether a school has a block schedule or a six- or seven-period day is less important than the quality of instruction. At a district level, whether a school board is appointed or elected is not as important as whether the district has a coherent curriculum and a [teacher] development plan that supports the curriculum.

There are so many different strategies that schools are using to improve. How do you replicate what a good school is doing if each school is doing something different?

What I tried to do in my book is give a clear vision so that other schools can say, "Oh, that makes sense, we could try to do something like that." That's my hope. Schools like to do things their own way. Some schools like before-school tutoring, some others like to do it after school. As long as the essential work is being done, as long as kids are learning, I think it's a good thing for schools to invent their own wheel.

If I'm a principal of a school with predominantly poor students or students of color, how do I know if my school is in a position to "get it done?"

The first thing you need to do is get a really clear vision of what your kids are supposed to know and do, and get a really clear look at where your school is in helping them. Then stop all talk about blaming the kids—don't even allow this to happen.

So that means a lot depends on you. You need knowledge, skill, and the ability to motivate people with a vision for where your school can go. Some of the principals I talked to who had the least experience went and visited a school that was performing better than their school and got as much advice as they could. Many took their teachers on field trips to those schools so that the teachers could see new possibilities. It seems to me that all schools are in a position to get it done. The question is whether the grown-ups are.

This chapter originally appeared in the May/June 2007 issue of the Harvard Education Letter.

PART IV

School and Community

CHAPTER 14

"R" is for Resilience

**Schools turn to "asset development"
to build on students' strengths**

by Nancy Walser

I magine a teenager as a balloon. One minute it's soaring; the next it's floating toward the ground, heading for a crash. But suppose there's an adult standing nearby who is willing to reach out and give it a gentle bop to send it soaring again? Better yet, what if there are five adults standing in a circle holding a thick web made of yarn? The tighter the web, the less likely the balloon can slip through and hit the ground.

This web-of-yarn exercise was invented by Derek Peterson, an educational consultant and one-man crusader who travels the globe preaching the benefits of youth development to teachers, administrators, school board members, and community leaders. The web—he likens it to a Lakota "dream-catcher"—is meant to demonstrate the impact of adult intervention in supporting resilience among teens.

Rather than focus on negative behaviors like acting out, drinking, or doing drugs, Peterson and others in the field of youth development are educating adults about "protective factors" and "developmental assets"—the positive attributes, experiences, and attitudes that 30 years of research shows are essential to children's success in school and in life. And they are finding a growing audience, both among administrators who are searching for new ways to motivate and engage teens and among test-weary staffers eager for the pendulum to swing back to a focus on the whole child.

A resurgence of interest in healthy social and emotional development can be seen across the country: from the state of Illinois, which enacted grade-level learning standards for social and emotional development in 2004, to Colorado, which has a statewide youth-development office called Assets for Colorado Youth, and up to Alaska, where the Association of Alaska School Boards has been working with school districts and other organizations since 1995 to get adults more involved in schoolchildren's everyday lives. Through student surveys, focus groups, "relationship plans," and other activities, school personnel are looking for ways to lay the groundwork for a lifetime of achievement and success.

BEYOND RISK PREVENTION

It wasn't so long ago that resilience—the ability to rise above adversity and thrive—was thought to be something a person was just born with. But recent research, including developmental psychologist Emmy Werner's longitudinal study of 698 Hawaiian children born in 1955, has identified key factors that resilient individuals have in common. In contrast to the risk-prevention approach, which concentrates on identifying "at-risk" youth and teaching them to avoid negative behaviors, asset development accentuates positive traits, behaviors, and attitudes and seeks to build on those.

At the forefront of this movement is the nonprofit Minneapolis-based Search Institute, where researchers Peter Benson and Peter Scales have combed through decades of research on resiliency, prevention, and adolescent development to identify 40 positive "assets" and arrange them in a user-friendly framework. Schools and other community organizations can use the framework to measure the collective strengths of their students and see how well these institutions support student resiliency.

Half of these factors are external, such as whether or not a child gets support from family members and three or more unrelated adults, while half are internal, such as whether or not a student cares about school and is motivated to do well. The assets are broadly grouped into eight categories: those that contribute to student support, empowerment, boundaries and expectations, constructive use of time, commitment to learning, positive values, social competencies, and positive identity.

Since 1996, the Search Institute has surveyed 3 million students in grades 6–12 across the country and found a direct correlation between the number of assets a student has and "thriving behaviors," such as getting mostly As on report cards or exhibiting leadership skills. The more assets a teenager has, the less likely he or she is to participate in high-risk behaviors, such as substance abuse, sex, and violence. These correlations are consistent for adolescents regardless of race, ethnicity, gender, age, socioeconomic background, community size, or region, according to the researchers.

More importantly, nearly all of these assets, if missing from a child's life, can be "built through concerted effort by schools and communities," according to Benson. He has identified 22 assets that schools can influence directly (see "Asset Checklist," p. 118).

"We have always known that human development is inextricably linked with academic development," Benson says, "but in a time in history where we are putting so much emphasis on testing and academic achievement, we risk losing sight of something that is very obvious: Achievement is as much about student development as it is about rigor and curriculum."

Communities that have been successful in building assets among youth are usually those where leaders like the school superintendent, the mayor, or the Chamber of Commerce president "use the bully pulpit to get it going," says Benson.

While the institute pushes asset-building initiatives that target community leaders as the most effective approach to building resiliency, the approach is also popular in schools. Sixty percent of the nearly 50,000 people trained by the organization in the last two years were school personnel, according to Mary Ackerman, director of external relations at the Search Institute.

Clay Roberts, a senior consultant who has trained administrators and teachers in more than 100 districts for the Search Institute, is seeing more and more Title I and Title II money going to training in asset development. "They really see the link between assets and achievement," he says. Asset development, he adds, is a tool for "engaging those who need to be engaged, whose scores are dragging everyone down."

The Search Institute works with schools in several ways. For example, it contracts with them to administer a 157-question student survey to determine the current level of assets among students, followed up by focus groups to clarify the survey's findings. It also trains administrators and staff in asset development; sponsors a listserv for more than 600 communities engaged in asset work; and hosts an annual conference to share strategies that have worked. Schools usually choose one or more assets to work on, using strategies that may include fundraising and community service projects; individual "strength interviews," in which advisors help students assess their own assets; or monthly relationship-building campaigns featuring banners that read HAVE LUNCH WITH ME AND FIND OUT

WHO I AM. Follow-up surveys help school personnel measure progress.

At the heart of this work is the effort to connect children with adults, says Ackerman. "Gates has his R for rigor; ours is for relationships. This is about adults changing so they can be more empowering for kids."

BUILDING ASSETS IN ALASKA

In Alaska, the school board association adopted the asset-development approach in a big way, funneling $2 million per year in funds designated for Native American achievement through No Child Left Behind to school districts and other organizations over a seven-year period for asset-building activities. As the director of child and youth advocacy for the association, Peterson cowrote a book, *Helping Kids Succeed—Alaskan Style*, which lists concrete ways that families, schools, religious, tribal, and community organizations can help children develop each of the 40 assets.

While the results are difficult to measure, in Anchorage, the state's largest district, SAT scores are rising steadily, 17 of 21 Title I schools made AYP last year, and drug use is down compared to the national average. "There are a lot of good things to point to," says Sally Rue, director of the Alaska Initiative for Community Engagement at the Association of Alaska School Boards.

Principal Darrell Vincek of the Willard L. Bowman Elementary School in Anchorage infuses asset-building into almost everything the school does. Every year at Bowman, staffers participate in "silent mentoring," an activity that begins with writing the name of every student on a paper star and posting it on "The Wall of Stars." Staffers then post their own names on stickies next to the name of any child with whom they have a significant relationship—someone they connect with on a regular basis or who could be counted on to come to them with a problem.

"What we found," says Vincek, "is that some kids have lots of adults in their lives, and there are kids in our building that nobody has a relationship with. Nobody!" Every staff member

ASSET CHECKLIST

The Search Institute has identified 22 assets that schools can influence to help their students become more resilient. How well do you think your school supports each of these?

Other adult relationships. Young person receives support from three or more nonparent adults.

Caring student climate. School provides a caring, encouraging environment.

Parent involvement in schooling. Parents are actively involved in helping young person succeed in school.

Community values youth. Young person perceives that adults in the community value youth.

Youth as resources. Young people are given useful roles in the community.

Service to others. Young person serves in the community one hour or more per week.

Safety. Young person feels safe at home, at school, and in neighborhood.

School boundaries. School provides clear rules and consequences.

Adult role models. Parent(s) and other adults model positive, responsible behavior.

Positive peer influence. Young person's best friends model responsible behavior.

volunteers to check in with one or two of these students by striking up a casual conversation periodically.

Students are also asked to write a letter every quarter to one significant adult at Bowman to thank that adult for "being a presence in their lives." Students deliver the letters to

High expectations. Both parent(s) and teachers encourage the young person to do well.

Creative activities. Young person spends three or more hours per week in lessons or practice in music, theater, or other arts.

Youth programs. Young person spends three or more hours per week in sports, clubs, or organizations at school and/or in the community.

Achievement motivation. Young person is motivated to do well in school.

School engagement. Young person is actively engaged in learning.

Homework. Young person reports doing at least one hour of homework every school day.

Bonding to school. Young person cares about her or his school.

Reading for pleasure. Young person reads for pleasure three or more hours per week.

Planning and decisionmaking. Young person knows how to plan ahead and make choices.

Interpersonal competence. Young person has empathy, sensitivity, and friendship skills.

Resistance skills. Young person can resist negative peer pressure and dangerous situations.

Peaceful conflict resolution. Young person seeks to resolve conflict nonviolently.

recipients, and copies are posted in the hallways. Staffers who get letters are often in tears, while those who don't get any or get only a few—well, it's a chance for a little self-reflection, says Vincek.

In a 2005 survey, 35 percent of Bowman students strongly agreed that "adults in my community support this school," compared with 15 percent districtwide. Forty percent strongly agreed that "there is at least one adult at this school whom I feel comfortable talking to about things that are bothering me," compared with 27 percent districtwide.

"We know if kids are connected to schools, they are going to do better, they are going to get their homework in," says Vincek. "These things don't take a lot of time."

ENGAGEMENT LEVELS, RELATIONSHIP PLANS

At the Search Institute, it's Roberts's job to train administrators and teachers how to do things differently in the time they have with students. It's not as easy as it sounds.

Based on his observations, Roberts classified six levels of ability among teachers to engage their students, ranging from the simple "Good morning, how are you?" to higher levels of involvement that give teachers the leverage to influence achievement and other good outcomes for kids. He encourages teachers to take a personal interest in each student, to find out their interests and aspirations, strengths, and talents. The most advanced teachers keep in touch with students over time, he says.

Roberts also works with teachers to make "relationship plans" in addition to regular lesson plans in order to identify potential barriers to connecting with certain students. "You need to get close, very close to those who you think will be the most difficult right away," he advises, "because when you need to discipline them—and you will—they will think you're doing it because you like them. The tendency is to do the opposite."

One reason why educators could be reluctant to get closer to students is explained by a call one Alaska superintendent received from a former student in South Dakota. The student had tracked the superintendent down at his new job in a district on a small island in Alaska to tell him that the student's brother had died. At the end of the conversation, the young man asked, "When are you coming back?"

"There are wonderful, wonderful highs with this work, but it can also be painful," the superintendent notes.

Meanwhile, Peterson continues weaving his web in Arizona, where the state school board association is working on a youth development project similar to Alaska's. "What I am trying to do is create space for very busy people to remember the basic principles of child and youth development," says Peterson. "This is a common sense–based framework with measurable outcomes so that people can come together with common goals for behavior that we'd like to see in classrooms, families, and communities."

This chapter originally appeared in the September/October 2006 issue of the Harvard Education Letter.

FOR FURTHER INFORMATION

B. Benard. *Resiliency: What We Have Learned*. San Francisco, CA: WestEd, 2004.

P. Benson. *All Kids Are Our Kids: What Communities Must Do to Raise Caring and Responsible Children and Adolescents*. San Francisco, CA: Jossey-Bass, 2006.

Initiative for Community Engagement (Alaska ICE), a Statewide Initiative of the Association of Alaska School Boards, 1111 West 9th St., Juneau, AK 99801; tel.: (907) 586-1083. www.alaskaice.org

The Search Institute, 615 First Ave. N.E., Suite 125, Minneapolis, MN 55413; tel.: (800) 888-7828. www.search-institute.org

N. Starkman, P. Scales, and C. Roberts. *Great Places to Learn: How Asset-Building Schools Help Students Succeed*. Minneapolis, MN: Search Institute, 1999.

CHAPTER 15

Reinforcement, Richness, and Relationships: The Three Rs of One Model Afterschool Program

A Boston program looks beyond tutoring and homework help to build student success

by Andreae Downs

Three well-scrubbed eighth graders sit around a conference table at the Richard J. Murphy School in Boston and politely explain why they come to Prime Time, the Murphy's afterschool program: homework help.

"My parents can't really help me; the work is new for them," says Gerald. If he couldn't go to Prime Time, he adds, "I'd be frustrated at home. It would be difficult for me to do my work."

Nick agrees: "All the teachers stay, so if you don't understand the assignment, you can go talk to the teacher that assigned it."

Stephanie says that if she went home to do homework she'd experience a lot more computer crashes, and she wouldn't have the library nearby.

But is homework help the *real* reason these students come to Prime Time?

"Well, it *is* fun," Stephanie finally admits. "Especially the dance classes and science experiments, or projects on ecosystems," she adds enthusiastically. Gerald likes "playing football with the boys, or basketball" on Fridays and "doing art" on Thursdays. Nick likes Destination ImagiNation®, a creativity and problem-solving program whereby teachers step back from instruction while children solve a particular problem or create something new—projects ranging from a model rocket to a play.

All three students also say they like the people and the atmosphere at Prime Time. "One reason I like to be here is the first time I came, everyone was friendly—the teachers, the kids, everyone," Gerald says.

A COMPREHENSIVE APPROACH

Prime Time has been a central component of principal Mary Russo's efforts to improve academic achievement at the 950-student Murphy, Boston's largest K–8 public school. So far these efforts have shown some remarkable results. When Russo arrived at the school in 1999, 58 percent of fourth graders failed the math portion of the Massachusetts Comprehensive Assessment System (MCAS), the state's standardized achievement test, and one in three could not read at grade level. Now the Murphy's fourth graders have the third-highest MCAS scores in Boston, and more than 90 percent pass both the math and English/language arts portions of the test.

In addition, Russo herself has received statewide and national recognition as an instructional leader. This year she was named one of five National Distinguished Principals by the National Association of Elementary School Principals, and she was named the 2004 Massachusetts Principal of the

Year by Boston's After-School for All Partnership, a public-private venture to promote high-quality before- and afterschool programs in the city.

Russo is the first to admit that the Murphy's extensive afterschool program is not the only reason for her students' success. She cites the expansion of the school to a K–8 (from a K–5), along with districtwide efforts to expand professional development and improve math and language arts curricula, as other keys to the school's turnaround. But the Murphy's heavy emphasis on afterschool is clearly one factor that has made it stand out as a local, state, and even national model. And Russo believes that the secret of Prime Time's success lies in the comprehensiveness of its approach to supporting student success.

Those who visit Prime Time in the early afternoon will see students receiving homework help in group or one-on-one tutoring. What they won't see is how focused the program is on reinforcing the work students do during the regular school day, and on building effective working relationships among students and the Murphy faculty. Murphy teachers staff Prime Time and maintain regular communication with each child's daytime teachers. Tutors are either Murphy teachers or Murphy interns—the school makes extensive use of students in local teacher-education programs—and afterschool program director Jonna Casey shares Russo's office. School rules on behavior also apply in Prime Time.

Besides an hour or so of daily homework time and tutoring as needed, Prime Time gives students an opportunity to participate in a variety of enrichment activities and includes a strong arts component. The program offers instrumental music lessons, dance classes, a variety of clubs, and art instruction. Students interested in admission to the city's arts high school can develop a portfolio. Prime Time also includes occasional field trips and special programs run by outside agencies like Historic New England, the nation's oldest and largest regional preservation program. Facilitators from Historic New England bring in actual and re-created artifacts, explain their relevance to their former owners, and ask students to reflect on and respond to the works in art and in writing.

Prime Time also includes another enrichment component whereby students are introduced to adults representing a variety of different professions. Staff from the National Wildlife Federation, for instance, provide a six-week environmental unit, and volunteers from the Boston Architects Association come to Prime Time and work with the children on design projects.

"This is time for children to capture the excitement of learning," says Russo. She adds that the program gives children many enrichment opportunities they might not otherwise have, and that these experiences can often spark a passion for learning that spills over into the school day.

Russo says the Murphy's Prime Time program also gives her and her afterschool faculty the opportunity to develop closer working relationships with parents. Because of budget constraints there are no afterschool buses, so many parents come by the school to pick up their children.

"This is the happiest time of day for me. I can meet the parents, buttonhole them. It improves communication," Russo says.

And Russo and her students aren't the only fans of Prime Time. Richard Murnane, an economist at the Harvard Graduate School of Education who has recently conducted extensive research in the Boston Public Schools, says the kinds of skills developed in programs like Prime Time are among those most in demand in today's job market. These include creating a project to test a hypothesis, active listening, working with others, social skills, presentation skills, and knowing how to work with common computer programs. Standardized tests are incapable of measuring most of these skills, Murnane notes, yet they can be of tremendous value, particularly to low-income children who may otherwise have few opportunities to develop them.

BUILDING SUPPORT FOR AFTERSCHOOL

Russo has long been a champion of afterschool programs, since well before they were fashionable, she says. In 1990, Russo faced an uphill battle but ultimately succeeded in starting an afterschool program at the school she previously led, the Samuel W. Mason School in Boston's Roxbury neighborhood. The Mason was one of the least-selected schools in Boston's school choice program and was in danger of closing when Russo arrived. By 1997 the school was considered a model and was named a Blue Ribbon School of Excellence by the U.S. Department of Education and a Title 1 Distinguished School, in part because of its highly effective afterschool program.

The Mason's two-hour program, which employed both teachers and volunteers from the AmeriCorps youth program City Year, soon grew from its first two classes of 15 students each to a much larger afterschool program and six-week summer camp. In addition to its original focus on homework and literacy, the expanded program included a variety of enrichment opportunities as well as experimental instruction and curriculum.

By 1999, when Russo arrived at the Murphy, afterschool was an easier sell. She had the support of parents, community institutions, the mayor, and the school department to start a program that would be an integral part of the school's improvement effort. Other city departments had realized that youth crime peaked in the afterschool hours and had made more funds available for child care. In the meantime, Boston's service providers had moved toward a model of delivering the needed services within schools, and private funders such as the Nellie Mae Education Foundation had commissioned research that confirmed the academic and social benefits of quality programs outside of school hours.

"In 1990 the atmosphere for afterschool was discouraging, and we were out on a limb," Russo says, recalling how little financing was available and how some school officials disparaged a number of her ideas. "Now people are celebrated for doing afterschool."

ACCOUNTABILITY FOR AFTERSCHOOL

Afterschool programs have been in existence for about 130 years and have varied widely in format and intent, according to Robert Halpern, a professor at the Erikson Institute, a graduate school in child development, and author of the book *Making Play Work: The Promise of After-School Programs for Low-Income Children*. As a result of the recent nationwide focus on standards and measurable academic achievement, afterschool has gotten additional attention and funding from both government and nonprofit sources, notes Crisanne L. Gayl, a researcher with the Progressive Policy Institute. In addition, afterschool has taken on a more academic focus in many schools, based on the notion that the programs offer children more time to hone their skills and raise their academic achievement—as well as their test scores.

But the nature of afterschool programs—that they are voluntary, attendance can be sporadic, and activities are not necessarily geared toward the development of specific academic skills—has meant that hard evidence linking afterschool programs to better test scores is slim, according to Gayl. The dearth of such evidence—and a 2003 Mathematica study of 21st Century Community Learning Center programs that showed no academic achievement gains at all—was cited by former education secretary Rod Paige as a reason to cut $400 million in federal afterschool funding in 2004. Congress ultimately held the funding steady, but the findings nonetheless raised questions for some about whether the government's investment in afterschool was yielding tangible returns.

What seems clearer from the research, however, is that students' attitudes about school and various academic-related behaviors, such as turning in homework and showing up for school regularly, are improved when students regularly attend a quality afterschool program. Beth Miller's 2003 review of the research on afterschool programs for the Nellie Mae Education Foundation noted that program participation was linked to several important factors: children were more engaged in learning, finished homework more often and with more attention, had fewer absences, and had better relationships with adults and peers in their school environments.

Whether the Murphy's out-of-school programs, which also include a weekend test-prep program called Saturday Scholars and several summer programs, actually improve test scores and other academic outcomes has not been rigorously studied. Initial statistical analysis of the state achievement test indicates that none of the children who attend afterschool programs at the Murphy fall into the two lowest achievement categories. While school statisticians say it's unclear whether this is because of the additional attention and time students get in the afterschool program or because the students who enroll come from more motivated families, Russo clearly believes Prime Time makes the difference. "It's a kind of intervention [for lower-achieving students]," she says. "For these children, we would definitely recommend the afterschool program."

For children who need extra help—and even for those who don't—Prime Time is an incredible deal. The full fee for one student is $40 per year, $60 for two students or more from the same family. Afterschool programs in nearby suburbs can run $230 a month or more for the same number of hours. Private tutoring in the Boston area starts at $35 per hour. But because so many of the Murphy's students qualify for free or reduced-price lunch (73%), the afterschool program is eligible for a variety of private and public funding sources, which the program's directors actively pursue for its $480,000 annual budget.

Yet even at 307 students, about a third of the school's student population, Russo is still not satisfied with the Murphy's afterschool programs and wants them to have a much broader reach. "We want all children [involved in the programs]," she says. "They could have more time to learn, they could do more cultural activities, instrumental music, second languages. We could add more value to their education with more time."

Russo says she could enroll more children if their parents could pick them up at the end of the day. Because of Boston's 30-year-old desegregation plan, students are bused across the city to the Murphy, but many parents are unable to pick up their children at the Murphy either because they cannot make it to the school by the six-o'clock end time or they do not have a car.

Another issue that virtually every school with an afterschool program faces is the funding required for the extra teacher time, as well as maintaining instructional quality and preventing teacher burnout. Currently, many of the teachers who stay for Prime Time do so only a few days a week, since staying after school more often is difficult for teachers with a lot of additional responsibilities.

Despite these complications, however, Russo would like to see the program grow, and hopes eventually to add many of the enrichment opportunities currently available in suburban schools to Prime Time. For one thing, she would like to add more sports so that students like Gerald could have more options. "We have a tremendous field here," Russo says. "I would love to offer lacrosse to our kids."

This chapter originally appeared in the March/April 2005 issue of the Harvard Education Letter.

FOR FURTHER INFORMATION

C.L. Gayl. "After-School Programs: Expanding Access and Ensuring Quality." Washington, DC: Progressive Policy Institute Policy Report, July 2004.

R. Halpern. *Making Play Work: The Promise of After-School Programs for Low-Income Children.* New York: Teachers College Press, 2003.

T. Kane. "The Impact of After-School Programs." New York: William T. Grant Foundation, January 2004. Available online at www.wtgrantfoundation.org

B.M. Miller. "Critical Hours: Afterschool Program and Educational Success." Quincy, MA: Nellie Mae Education Foundation, May 2003. Available online at www.nmfdn.org

E.R. Reisner, R.N. White, C.A. Russell, and J. Birmingham. "Building Quality, Scale, and Effectiveness in After-School Programs." Washington, DC: Policy Studies Associates, Inc., November 2, 2004. Available online at www.policystudies.com

CHAPTER 16

Parents as Partners in School Reform

Outreach, training—and respect—are keys to tapping this critical source of support

by Nancy Walser

Jared Christensen is a real estate investor in the burgeoning suburbs of southern Salt Lake County. The father of four, he is also a parent representative on the community council at South Hills Middle School. He's not an expert on education, but two years ago, when then-principal Michael Sirois came to the council to talk about what adolescents need in school, how the school needed to change, and how parents could help, Christensen was intrigued.

"He talked to us about what it takes to handle a changing adolescent. They learn a little bit differently than an adult or younger child," Christensen recalls. Sirois also stressed the need for teachers to meet so they could talk about the progress of each child in every subject. To Christensen, that made a lot of sense. "Middle schoolers need a lot of support," he says.

For years before Sirois's appeal to his council, South Hills had been trying to switch from a junior high model to a middle school model better tailored to the needs of early adolescents. District administrators had studied a number of national middle school reform models and had encouraged teachers to implement some of the essential elements, such as teaming up with one another to get to know students better and develop more challenging, interdisciplinary curricula. But South Hills's reform efforts had hit a wall. With a high student-teacher ratio and one of the lowest per-pupil expenditures in the country, the school was struggling to find ways to create time for teachers to meet and collaborate.

If classes could end an hour and a half earlier once a week, teachers would have the critically needed time for team meetings. But for that to happen, Sirois felt, parents had to be on board. "My fear was that if we couldn't clearly convey to parents what we were trying to do and why, their natural concerns would turn to mistrust and opposition," he explains.

Armed with $90,000 in district pilot funding, Sirois invited professional development experts to talk to his faculty and council members about middle school philosophy and the importance of collaboration and teaming. Parents on the council were invited to all in-service sessions offered to faculty. Some parents took fact-finding trips to schools that had successfully implemented middle school reforms. Parent council members helped lead a half-dozen community meetings to present the planned changes to other parents. Finally, Sirois took the unorthodox step of asking parents to vote on the schedule change by secret ballot. Ninety-six percent of the parents voted in favor of the change, with 75 percent of families voting.

WINNING HEARTS AND MINDS

As pressure to raise student achievement continues to escalate, more eyes are turning to the role that parents can play in supporting, sustaining, and sometimes—as in the case of South Hills—even resuscitating reform efforts. "School leaders are beginning to realize that they can't do [school improvement] all by themselves," says Elena Lopez, a consultant to the Harvard Family Research Project who has studied parent engagement. "To succeed, they need the support of parents and the community."

In *The New Meaning of Educational Change*, Michael Fullan, dean of the Ontario Institute for Studies in Education of the University of Toronto and an expert on school change, cites 30 years of research consistently linking parent involvement with achievement. "Parents and other community members are crucial and largely untapped resources," he writes.

Indeed, the literature is full of cautionary tales for administrators attempting to lead school reform alone. For example, an April 2005 Colorado Small School Initiative evaluation of the four-year, $1 million effort to convert Denver's Manual High School into three small schools found that, in addition to other problems, "control of the change process in all three small schools was maintained by a few individuals," which "fostered mistrust and negatively affected motivation among students, parents, and teachers, reducing the probability that reforms will be successful." The report recommended that high schools attempting small-school reform should "build opportunities for families and the community to be engaged in the reform process from the very beginning, using real data about student performance."

Larry Myatt, director of the small-schools leadership project for the Greater Boston Principal Residency Network at Northeastern University, echoed these concerns in an *Education Week* editorial earlier this year. Myatt pointed to the lack of parental involvement as one of nine factors inhibiting efforts to establish small-school reform in U.S. high schools, despite considerable funding.

"One lesson we have learned for certain in small-learning-community conversion work is that, if we don't win the hearts and minds of the people involved, things will stay as they are," he wrote. "There is also a history of asking families, particularly those in urban communities, to embrace the latest plan affecting their neighborhood schools only during its latter stages, rather than asking them to be partners early on."

A CONTINUUM OF CHANGE

What worked for Sirois may not work for administrators in all districts. In particular, the challenges of engaging parents as partners in middle-class suburban schools may be very different from those of developing parent leadership in low-income or urban school districts.

"There are different ways that parents are participating in school reform," says Lopez, the research consultant. She notes that in many schools, particularly in low-income districts, the first step is to build positive relationships among parents, and between parents and school staff. "For parents to sustain [a high] level of participation and decisionmaking, they need a lot of training," she observes. "Once you get parents hooked about how, collectively, they have a lot of power to make changes in school, then you can do more formal training around school reform." She points to Marin County's Parent Service Project to illustrate this approach to training parent leaders.

The Parent Service Project (PSP), a national nonprofit organization dedicated to encouraging family participation in preschools and schools, operates 700 programs in eight states. In Marin County, Calif., supported by the private Marin Community Foundation, PSP is helping parents organize to improve student achievement in eight low-income elementary schools. PSP provides child care, coaching, and training for parents and facilitates meetings to bring parents and staff together to solve problems and support the academic goals of their school.

**SELECTED GUIDELINES FOR FOSTERING
PARENT LEADERSHIP**

- State explicitly your school's high expectations for parent participation.
- Engage parents in developing a shared vision for all students.
- Make learning transparent: Keep classrooms open for visits; hold "walkthroughs" with parents; discuss how learning occurs and how it can be recognized.
- Develop structures and processes for parent-to-parent leadership, such as phone trees for opinion polling and information sharing.
- Assume that parents have the right, responsibility, and ability to struggle with tough issues.
- Keep parent participation broad based; do whatever it takes (e.g., provide translation services, babysitting, or food) to involve a wide spectrum of parents.

Adapted from Linda Lambert, Leadership Capacity for Lasting School Improvement *(Alexandria, VA: ASCD, 2003).*

In 2001, for example, PSP training and program director Mauricio Palma met with parents at San Pedro Elementary School in San Rafael to translate and discuss a newspaper article that identified their school as one of the lowest-scoring schools in the county. Parent leaders at the school decided to host a soccer tournament to reach out to other parents and build interest in the school. As interest grew, parents worked with school staff to lobby the district for a new cafeteria and fulfilled a teacher's wish for a classroom garden. At the same time, Palma worked with the school principal to identify and invite parent leaders to join the site-based management council. The following year, parents were involved in setting academic and nonacademic goals for the school and monitoring the school's progress in achieving them.

Achievement at San Pedro Elementary, as measured by the California Academic Performance Index, has increased every year since 2002. The school has also exceeded its state performance targets for the last three consecutive years—a situation that Don Jen, program officer at the Marin Community Foundation, attributes partly to the hiring of a literacy coach and partly to increased parent engagement.

THE ROLE OF THE PRINCIPAL

In many schools, however, parents are only as effective as school leaders allow them to be. In *Leadership Capacity for Lasting School Improvement*, Linda Lambert, a former middle school principal and professor emeritus at California State University, Hayward, distinguishes between parent involvement and parent leadership. She notes that principals tend to treat parents as customers to be satisfied rather than as partners engaged in a common task, and often hesitate to share with them information that might not be positive or ideas that are still being explored. Parents, meanwhile, may need guidance to move from concern for their own children to concern for all children.

"Parents may start out thinking their children are the most important thing, and yet, they can end up saying, 'I'm concerned about all the students in the school'—if they are engaged in conversation," she says.

To allay fears about parents' overstepping their roles, Lambert recommends that principals set boundaries at the beginning. Teacher evaluations and personnel matters are off limits, for example. "If it's open season, there will be parents who come into the group with their own agenda," she says. (See "Selected Guidelines for Fostering Parent Leadership," p. 137.)

MEASURING THE IMPACT

It's difficult to measure the effects of parental support on school performance, given the number of variables involved. Nonetheless, observers like Lambert and Lopez say schools that have worked to engage parents in reform efforts typically see positive results. Sirois, the former principal at South Hills Middle School, notes that since the new schedule was implemented, the district and state have twice changed the annual tests used to measure student achievement. "But I can tell you that even though we increased the rigor of required classes, the number of students failing a class has decreased dramatically," he says.

Surveys show that South Hills parents are satisfied as well. And when its school district announced plans to open another middle school this fall, parents requested that the new middle school use the same schedule as South Hills, including the weekly early release for teacher meetings.

"We came up with this idea," says Sirois, who will take up the principalship at the new middle school, "but we realized we needed to include parents from the beginning. Most parents come with their own ideas and their own agendas. You can't just tell them and expect them to understand. The best way is to get them in your school to see what you are trying to do."

This chapter originally appeared in the September/October 2005 issue of the Harvard Education Letter.

FOR FURTHER INFORMATION

M.E. Lopez and H. Kreider. "Beyond Input: Achieving Authentic Participation in School Reform." *The Evaluation Exchange* 9, no. 2 (Summer 2003). Available online at www.gse.harvard.edu/hfrp/eval/issue22/theory.html

Harvard Family Research Project. "Program Spotlight: Parent Services Project." *FINE Forum e-Newsletter* 8 (Spring 2004). Available online at www.gse.harvard.edu/hfrp/projects/fine/fineforum/forum8/spotlight.html

H.C. Giles. "Parent Engagement as a School Reform Strategy." *ERIC Digests.org.* Available online at www.ericdigests.org/1998-3/reform.html

M. Fullan. *The New Meaning of Educational Change*, 3rd ed. New York: Teachers College Press, 2001.

L. Lambert. *Leadership Capacity for Lasting School Improvement*. Alexandria, VA: Association for Supervision and Curriculum Development, 2003.

National Association of Elementary School Principals. "Leading Learning Communities: Standards for What Principals Should Know and Be Able to Do." Alexandria, VA: Author, 2001. Executive summary available online at www.ecs.org/html/Document.asp?chouseid=3392

PART V

Leading for Change

CHAPTER 17

Beyond Bargaining

What does it take for school district–union collaboration to succeed?

by Mitch Bogen

ast spring, teachers in San Francisco and Oakland
threatened their first strike since 1979. In Detroit, 1,500
teachers in more than 50 schools participated in an un-
official "sickout" over salary issues. In a climate of fi-
nancial constraint and escalating pressure to meet the federal
mandates of the No Child Left Behind Act (NCLB), tensions
between school district management and teachers unions ap-
pear to be rising nationwide.

But at the same time, in districts across the country, these
traditional foes have been working together to implement
collaborative reforms. From merit pay systems to peer review programs, innovations designed to improve the quality
of teaching and learning in classrooms have been introduced
into today's collective bargaining agreements.

As public schools face NCLB-related takeover and turnaround plans on the one hand and choice options like charter
schools and vouchers on the other, it's imperative that districts and unions continue to rethink the idea that "their interests are oppositional by nature," says Paul Reville, execu-

143

tive director of the Rennie Center for Education Research & Policy, which sponsors forums on labor-management relationships for district-level managers and labor leaders. "It's in all our interests to think together and work collaboratively to improve performance in this sector, or we're eventually going to lose the franchise," he adds.

Many educators say that focusing on student achievement is the best way to stimulate productive district-union collaboration. In fact, says Adam Urbanski, president of the Rochester (N.Y.) Teachers Association and director of the Teacher Union Reform Network (TURN), "it's not only the best way, it's the only way. There is no other common denominator that can bind us together."

Susan Moore Johnson, a professor of teaching and learning at the Harvard Graduate School of Education who has written about unions and teacher quality, cautions that accountability pressures can also create disincentives for collaboration. "I would say that collaborative work is not flourishing," she says. In districts where budgets are tight or where pressure for improvement results in a "top-down" management style, she says, "it's very hard to maintain collaborative approaches."

How can administrators and union leaders work together to lay the groundwork for collaboration? As districts and unions gain experience implementing innovative practices aimed at improving teacher quality and supporting student achievement, they have begun to identify some of the building blocks that lead to successful working relationships.

INNOVATIVE PRACTICES

"Working together for the purpose of improving student learning is possible," emphasizes Linda Kaboolian, author of *Win-Win Labor-Management Collaboration in Education*, published by the Rennie Center in cooperation with Education Week Press. The book cites examples of district-union collaboration across the country, such as provisions that allow for extended school days and school years, agreements that give schools more control over teacher hiring, assignment, and transfer, or pay-for-performance programs that tie teacher compensation to student achievement and other related factors.

One of the best-known and longest-standing examples of district-union collaboration is the peer review and evaluation program known as the Toledo Plan. Established more than 20 years ago in Toledo, Ohio, the plan gave teachers the power to recommend termination of fellow teachers. "Were we actually giving up power?" asks Craig Cotner, Toledo's former chief academic officer. "In the five years prior to implementing the plan, the district terminated one teacher. Since the Toledo Plan there have been over 400 teachers nonrenewed."

"The collaboration that is required to make the Toledo Plan operate fosters a sense of trust and mutual respect that carries over to other venues," Cotner adds.

Other districts with a shared focus on student achievement have also succeeded in implementing reforms using some innovative bargaining practices (see "Promising Practices in Contract Negotiation," p. 147). In Rochester, N.Y., known for its long-standing career ladder program, the union and district have negotiated contract-override provisions to allow flexibility in teacher assignment. Minneapolis's contract includes language acknowledging a commitment to student achievement and emphasizing school-based accountability and decisionmaking. The agreement establishes Professional Development Centers linked to student performance and outlines a process for identifying and working with struggling schools.

These kinds of systemic reforms usually occur only after districts and unions have first succeeded with a single negotiated reform, which fosters the trust needed to proceed with further collaboration, as in the cases of Toledo and Rochester.

Successful collaboration "does unleash all kinds of new energy into the system," says Kaboolian. Urbanski puts a different spin on it. "When all hell breaks loose," he says, "you're onto something real."

PROMOTING COLLABORATION

Still, collaborative reform isn't the norm. Both district staffers and union officials face pressures from their respective colleagues and constituents to "look tough" and "not sell out," Kaboolian says. When district staff find union leaders they can work with, she says, they should seize the opportunity. "Your job is to get as much done with them as possible and still allow them to maintain their political viability." If you don't, she adds, "the person who replaces them is most likely going to be a lot more difficult to work with." (See "Superintendents' Suggestions," p. 149.)

"You can't take collaboration for granted," she warns.

Many observers suggest that first steps toward collaboration are best taken outside the context of formal collective bargaining negotiations. "If there is a problem in the district that needs work, I would encourage [the district] to form a multi-stakeholder study group and learn about the topic and possible reform efforts together," says Kaboolian. These kinds of ventures can help build trust among the various parties, generate results that can win support for innovation, and lay the groundwork for the next steps.

For unions, emphasizing professionalism, as opposed to traditional bread-and-butter unionism, can galvanize support for collaborative reform among the rank and file, Urbanski suggests. Most reforms in Rochester, for example, have been designed to define and improve professional practice and accountability. The Rochester Teachers Association, he says, continually seeks to "assume responsibility for the quality of

PROMISING PRACTICES IN CONTRACT NEGOTIATION

Districts and unions across the country are experimenting with innovative bargaining methods. Some of the most promising practices include:

- "interest-based" bargaining, a less adversarial approach to negotiations that focuses on shared interests rather than fixed positions;

- contract waivers or overrides, in which both parties temporarily agree to sidestep existing provisions for specific, time-limited purposes;

- "living contracts," which allow continued renegotiation and modification to meet evolving circumstances; and

- "thin contracts," which address basic issues and set standard conditions at the district level, but allow more detailed supplemental contracts that affect day-to-day operations to be hammered out at the school site level.

Adapted from Win-Win Labor-Management Collaboration in Education: Breakthrough Practices to Benefit Students, Teachers, and Administrators, *by Linda Kaboolian, with Paul Sutherland (Mt. Morris, IL: The Rennie Center for Educational Research & Policy and Education Week Press, 2005).*

their members' work and for their ongoing professional development."

THE CASE OF PROCOMP

Perhaps the most dramatic example of successful union-district collaboration is in Denver, where a six-year process of experimentation and negotiation led to the development of the widely publicized ProComp pay-for-performance (PFP) plan, the most comprehensive such program in the nation. According to Andre Pettigrew, assistant superintendent for administrative services, and Bruce Dickinson, executive director of the Denver Classroom Teachers Association (DCTA), the process of collaborative negotiation featured several key characteristics that led to success. The process was:

Fully collaborative. Dickinson recalls that the district actually did try initially to launch the process with a unilateral proposal, "but we viewed that as coercive and said, 'No, a thousand times no.'" After reaching an impasse with the management and influenced by its participation in TURN, the DCTA saw the issue as a springboard for reform and proposed that the union and the district investigate it jointly. Over time, district officials and union leaders learned to "leave their hats at the door."

Well-researched, deliberate, and highly structured. The project began with a three-year pilot program to research the link between various measures of teacher performance and student achievement. Based on the results, the district formed a Joint Task Force on Teacher Compensation to develop a specific proposal for Denver.

Distinguished by choice and buy-in options. For Dickinson, it was critical that the pilot process feaure a strong element of buy-in. A school's participation in the pilot project had to be approved by 80 percent of its faculty. Schools that participated in the pilot could also choose one of three approaches to measuring changes in student achievement. Although new teachers are automatically enrolled in the ProComp program starting this fall, participation remains optional for veteran teachers.

Characterized by broad stakeholder input and support. "Typically, negotiations like these are bilateral," says Petti-

SUPERINTENDENTS' SUGGESTIONS

Former urban superintendents gave their peers the following advice at a recent colloquium regarding working with unions on education reform:

- Encourage collaboration around the "main thing"—student achievement. Ideally, the contract becomes a living document that adjusts and changes continually as understanding of student achievement evolves.
- Make the contract the instrument for advancing student learning. If it isn't in the contract, it's not really the main thing.
- Think of negotiating as a problem-solving mechanism, not a source of conflict. Ideally it should be a perpetual tool for problem-solving.
- Unions have an interest in good schools, too.
- Keep up to speed on what's happening with union reform. Some of the most progressive ideas about how to advance the learning are coming from union leaders themselves.

Reprinted with permission from Win-Win Labor-Management Collaboration in Education: Breakthrough Practices to Benefit Students, Teachers, and Administrators, *by Linda Kaboolian, with Paul Sutherland (Mt. Morris, IL: The Rennie Center for Educational Research & Policy and Education Week Press, 2005).*

grew. In Denver, however, foundations, business leaders, politicians, and community organizations played a strong role in developing the model, which encouraged community support for the project. In October 2005, Denver voters approved $25 million to fund the ProComp plan.

LEARNING THE RIGHT LESSON

Dickinson emphasizes that the lesson of ProComp for other districts is not "that you try [to replicate] it lock, stock, and barrel." Instead, he hopes people will learn from the process of collaboration.

That's an important distinction, according to Andrew Rotherham, codirector of the policy think tank Education Sector and coeditor of *Collective Bargaining in Education*, published in 2006 by Harvard Education Press, which analyzes the available research in this area. Too many people, he says, want to treat PFP as a kind of "litmus test" that proves whether others are "for or against" reform and innovation. This can limit district and union leaders' ability to find collaborations that will work best for their districts.

Successful collaboration does not spell the end of skepticism and antagonism in school districts. Dickinson concedes that ProComp remains controversial, despite being approved by a majority of union members. Nonetheless, with both the accountability movement and teachers unions firmly established as central forces in contemporary public education, confrontation seems increasingly impractical: time spent fighting the other side is time not spent on the improvement of teaching and learning. As Urbanski asserts: "No one should be surprised that before the kids can get their act together, the adults in their lives should be able to do so first."

This chapter originally appeared in the September/October 2006 issue of the Harvard Education Letter.

FOR FURTHER INFORMATION

Denver Public Schools Professional Compensation System for Teachers (Denver ProComp). www.denverprocomp.org

J. Hannaway and A. Rotherham, eds. *Collective Bargaining in Education: Negotiating Change in Today's Schools*. Cambridge, MA: Harvard Education Press, 2006.

L. Kaboolian, with P. Sutherland. *Win-Win Labor-Management Collaboration in Education: Breakthrough Practices to Benefit Students, Teachers, and Administrators.* Mt. Morris, IL: The Rennie Center for Educational Research & Policy and Education Week Press, 2005.

Rennie Center for Educational Research & Policy, 131 Mount Auburn St., 1st Floor, Cambridge, MA 02138; tel.: (617) 354-0992. www.renniecenter. org

Teacher Union Reform Network. www.turnexchange.net

The Toledo Plan. www.tft250.org/the_toledo_plan.htm

What (So-Called) Low-Performing Schools Can Teach (So-Called) High-Performing Schools

by Richard F. Elmore

My work as a researcher and consultant takes me into classrooms in all sorts of schools. My primary interest is improving the quality of teaching in high-poverty, racially diverse schools. Lately, however, I have also been called upon to visit schools in more affluent communities—some of them extraordinarily affluent.

While visiting schools in a variety of districts, I began to notice something that puzzled me. Some of these schools, particularly those with large numbers of poor and minority children, are working against daunting—some would say unreasonable—expectations for improvement in test scores. In more affluent schools, these pressures are much less evident. Yet the kinds of instructional problems that surface in both types of schools are strikingly similar.

In wealthy schools and poor ones, I encountered the same recurring patterns: considerable variation among classrooms in the degree to which students were challenged; an emphasis on procedural knowledge and factual recall at the expense of analysis, reflection, and understanding; a tendency to focus more on students who were "easy to teach" than on those who were struggling; and low estimates of students' capabilities. I also noticed that teachers tended to base their instruction on the level of challenge that they—as teachers—were most comfortable with, rather than what students could actually do.

Then, as part of my research on accountability, I began to examine *successful* schools with high concentrations of poor and minority children—those in which students were doing as well as or better than those in affluent schools on statewide standardized tests—to see what they were doing to improve the level of instruction in their classrooms. These high-performing, high-poverty schools were not just different in degree from other schools, they were *different in kind*. School leaders had clearly articulated expectations for student learning, coupled with a sense of urgency about improvement; they adopted challenging curricula and invested heavily in professional development. Teachers in these schools internalized responsibility for student learning; they examined their practices critically, and if they weren't working, they abandoned them and tried something else.

Most important, school leaders insisted that classrooms be open to teacher colleagues, administrators, and outsiders for observation and analysis of instructional practice. For instance, teachers might review test scores together to pinpoint content areas and classrooms where children seem to be struggling, and then observe the classrooms and discuss what changes in teaching practice might help these children succeed. Even high-poverty schools that were in the initial stages of improvement but still classified as "low-performing" seemed to be working in a different way than schools whose performance did not trigger adverse attention under the accountability requirements of the federal No Child Left Behind Act.

OUTSOURCING THE PROBLEM

When I returned to visit schools in more affluent communities, I began to see them in a very different light. On paper, these schools' performance usually looked reasonably good. From the inside, however, they looked jarringly different from the improving high-poverty schools I had observed.

One of the most powerful differences was that teachers and administrators tended to define student learning difficulties as a problem to be solved by students and their families, rather than one to be solved by schools. A common response to student learning problems in these districts is to suggest that parents seek private tutoring. At a recent gathering of about 300 educators from high-income schools and districts, I asked how many could tell me the proportion of students in their schools who were enrolled in private tutoring. Only four or five hands went up. But among those respondents, the answers ranged from 20 to 40 percent.

What does this mean for instructional improvement? These schools are outsourcing the task of teaching every student—and from classroom to classroom, teachers may not even be aware of it. As a result, teachers are not challenged to identify shortcomings in their own practice that inhibit student learning, or to share knowledge about which teachers are most successful and why.

In more affluent communities, I also found that variations in student performance were frequently taken for granted. Instead of being seen as a challenge to teachers' practice, these differences were used to classify students as more or less talented. Access to high-level courses was intentionally limited, reinforcing the view that talent, not instruction, was the basis of student achievement.

There were exceptions, of course—sometimes dramatic exceptions—to this general pattern, where teachers, principals, and superintendents were willing to challenge the conventional norms and expectations of high-performing schools and take a critical look at their own practice. Leaders in these schools question prevailing beliefs about the differences in student learning, stimulate discussion about the quality of student work, and—like their counterparts in less wealthy schools—focus on content areas where classroom work seems markedly below what students are capable of doing.

While the verdict is still out, I have noticed that challenging expectations in these schools often puts leaders in a risky place. Parents and school boards in affluent communities may not want to hear that the teaching in their schools is mediocre. The accountability system does not call attention to the problems of instructional quality in these schools, nor does it reinforce efforts to solve them. Improvement can be a dangerous business in settings like these, and some principals and superintendents have the scars to prove it. Unlike low-performing schools, which may be galvanized by external pressure to improve, so-called high-performing schools must often swim against a tide of complacency to generate support for change.

REWARDING THE WRONG THINGS

If existing accountability systems could actually measure the value that schools add to student learning, independent of family background, the schools now ranked as "high performing" would probably cleave into two categories: schools in which students' academic performance is related to the quality of teaching and learning, and schools in which performance is largely attributable to income and social class.

But standards-based accountability systems don't operate that way. They put all schools whose students perform at the same level into the same category, regardless of how they got there. Because the existing federal accountability system does not distinguish between schools that produce results through high-quality teaching and those that produce results largely through social class, it is largely rewarding the wrong things.

As an educator, I think we have much more to learn from studying high-poverty schools that are on the path to improvement than we do from studying nominally high-performing schools that are producing a significant portion of their performance through social class rather than instruction. Although these schools may be stigmatized as "low performing" or "in need of improvement," they are working hard to learn about their practice and beginning to focus on the individual and organizational conditions that create more powerful learning for adults and children. These nominally low-performing schools are, in most respects, the most interesting and powerful places to learn about learning.

This chapter originally appeared in the September/October 2005 issue of the Harvard Education Letter.

CHAPTER 19

In Praise of the Comprehensive High School

We can learn from what small schools do well—but there are things big schools can do better

by Laura Cooper

As an administrator in a large, comprehensive high school, I am often asked *when*—not *if*—we plan to break the school down into a number of small schools. Wouldn't forming small schools help us to close the gap in achievement between our white students and our African American and Latino students? I've come to the conclusion that forming many small schools is not the primary answer to the challenges faced by Evanston Township High School (ETHS). But I think there's a lot that schools like ETHS can learn from small schools.

Located in a multiracial suburb of Chicago, ETHS serves 3,200 students. The student body is 48 percent white, 39 percent African American, 10 percent Latino, and 2 percent Asian. About a third of the students are low-income. The school is part of the Minority Student Achievement Network (MSAN), a coalition of 25 multiracial, relatively affluent urban-suburban school districts across the nation that seek to ensure high academic achievement for students of color. Our commitment to narrowing the achievement gap requires us to pay careful attention to the research coming out of small schools. Nonetheless, my MSAN colleagues and I agree that dismantling schools like ours is not the place to start.

DIVERSITY AND CITIZENSHIP

The high schools in MSAN districts such as Madison, Shaker Heights, Chapel Hill, and Ann Arbor have helped to define academic excellence. They regularly receive kudos for their national award-winning student debaters, math teams, and theatrical or musical groups, and display proudly their long lists of National Merit scholars. MSAN high schools exemplify the widely acknowledged strengths of a large school—the ability to offer a comprehensive curriculum, including career programs, an array of AP classes, and programs for English-language learners, as well as the ability to create a wide variety of extracurricular and athletic opportunities. All of these are advantages few smaller schools can match. But our reluctance to break large comprehensive high schools into small schools is also tied to our historical commitment to racial, ethnic, and linguistic diversity.

Many MSAN communities voluntarily desegregated their schools in the late sixties and the early seventies. While these communities have welcomed increasing numbers of African American, Latino, and other nonwhite students, the districts have maintained a significant percentage of white students. Today, MSAN districts are anomalies in a nation whose schools are increasingly segregated by race and income level. Working together since 1999, these schools have made a shared commitment to diversity, to closing gaps in achievement, and to preparing all students for college, work, and citizenship.

Participation in a large and diverse school community is one of the best ways to prepare students for citizenship and work in a multicultural society. A school large enough to include all the racial, ethnic, and linguistic groups in the district can offer a wide variety of courses that can help prepare students for life in a multicultural society—for instance, courses in sociology, African history, or Japanese. But the most powerful lessons students learn are from the daily experience of getting to know each other in the context of intellectual inquiry, athletic competitions, artistic performances, and community service. When asked about their experiences with racial and ethnic diversity, 12th graders at Cambridge (Mass.) Rindge and Latin High School (an MSAN district) reported a strong level of comfort with members of other racial and ethnic groups. More importantly, students reported that because of their school experiences, they had an increased level of understanding of diverse points of view and a greater desire to interact with people of different backgrounds in the future.

The caution about small schools is based in part on lessons learned from some early efforts to create small schools within a larger school, in which student and parent choice led to "balkanized" small schools, each dominated by one racial, linguistic, or income group, in which students (and parents) lost a sense of belonging to a larger school community. More recent research indicates that while small schools are often successful at strengthening personal relationships, their impact on achievement is mixed, particularly in schools created by redesigning a larger school.

When MSAN school leaders have moved in the direction of small school reform, they have done so with caution. For instance, when administrators in Madison, Montclair, and Cleveland Heights designed smaller learning communities within their large high schools, they developed structures and policies to maintain diversity in classes and programs. They also made special efforts to balance the personalization of a small community with a sense of belonging to the larger school community.

LESSONS FROM SMALL SCHOOLS

Small schools may not be *the* answer for ETHS or other MSAN high schools, but, ironically, the experiments going on in small city schools may be our best source of ideas for ways to improve student achievement. There are two compelling reasons for learning from our urban colleagues. First, we share some common challenges: Suburban schools also serve students who feel disengaged and anonymous, and who are unprepared for the academic demands of high school–level work. Second, small schools are the only places where researchers are studying what works in high school reform. Recent studies conducted in small schools offer insights into three challenges faced by all high schools: how to create a personalized learning environment for all students; how to accelerate the learning of students who enter high school below grade level; and how to improve instruction by creating professional communities among teachers.

Personalized learning. High school leaders know that students are more likely to succeed academically in an environment of close interpersonal relationships and mutual respect. While creating a personalized learning environment is well documented as a strength of newly created small high schools, schools don't have to be small to do what these schools are doing. Successful strategies include academies (often a freshman academy followed by a three-year career academy); faculty advisory systems; and special classes for academic support. Like many MSAN schools, ETHS has created an advisory program in which one adult and a small group of students meet almost daily over a four-year period, along with other small, supportive communities such as the Advancement Via Individual Determination (AVID) program or Project Excel.

Academic preparation. Students often enter high school poorly prepared for a rigorous curriculum. Recent research points to the need for an intensive focus on ninth graders as they make the transition from middle to high school. Large schools might borrow the "on track" indicator developed by the Consortium on Chicago School Research (CCSR) to monitor student progress. This makes possible early intervention to provide the supports needed to get students "on track" to meet high academic expectations and fulfill increasingly stringent graduation requirements.

Large schools might also learn from the Talent Development Model's Ninth Grade Success Academy, which provides double classes of English/reading and mathematics and offers explicit instruction in academic and social skills. Many MSAN schools are designing and implementing double-period math and literacy classes. At ETHS, students who read significantly below grade level participate in a double-period Read 180 class and work with English and history teachers who integrate literacy instruction into the curriculum. Students who are not prepared for algebra are assigned to a double-period Algebra 1 class that includes a focused curriculum, reteaches basic skills, and uses AgileMind software that emphasizes problem-solving and conceptual understanding. About 40 students each year do so well that we accelerate their math trajectory by teaching a year of geometry in summer school so that they will be on track to take calculus senior year.

Building a professional community. We know that there is a strong relationship between professional teacher community and student achievement. Many schools have organized high school teachers into teams that share the same students or that teach the same content. But how can we ensure that the conversations within those teams lead to collective changes in instruction?

A recent CCSR study looks inside teacher teams and distinguishes between "supportive" activities that address immediate concerns (help with an individual student or assisting a new teacher with planning a lesson) and "developmental" activities that lead to sustained improvements in instruction. The researchers found that the small urban schools studied were characterized by "supportive" rather than "developmental" activities—perhaps because it's easier for members of the group to support a colleague than to make collective decisions to teach core content in a different way.

Drawing on these findings, ETHS has restructured our staff development and meeting time to connect our work on professional community more directly with our goal of improving student achievement. We will ensure that our professional learning communities receive support in analyzing assessment data (including student work) to improve instruction.

Schools like ETHS are vestiges of an earlier era. Given all the research now available to us, few people founding a school today would set out to create a school with 3,200 students. Over the years, however, schools like ETHS have come to take on a central, unifying role in their communities. The culture that grows up within and around these schools serves their students well. In many cases, breaking these large schools into smaller schools would sacrifice hard-earned strengths while offering few compensating advantages. Nonetheless, administrators in large, comprehensive high schools can find in the research that comes out of the small schools movement both inspiration and insights for making our own schools more successful. Whether high schools are small, large, or somewhere in between, we are all tackling the same tough issues.

We should set aside the traditional boundaries that have separated us—urban or suburban, homogenous or diverse, large or small—and begin to learn from each other.

This chapter originally appeared in the September/October 2006 issue of the Harvard Education Letter.

FOR FURTHER INFORMATION

Evanston Township High School, 1600 Dodge Ave., Evanston, IL 60204; tel.: (847) 424-7000. www.eths.k12.il.us

Gates Foundation Small School Initiative, Bill & Melinda Gates Foundation, P.O. Box 23350, Seattle, WA 98102; tel.: (206) 709-3100. www.gatesfoundation.org

Minority Student Achievement Network, 1600 Dodge Ave., Evanston, IL 60204; tel.: (847) 424-7185. www.msanetwork.org

CHAPTER 20

The Road to School Improvement

It's hard, it's bumpy, and it takes as long as it takes

by Richard F. Elmore and Elizabeth A. City

In our work on instructional improvement with low-performing schools, we are often asked, "How long does it take?" The next most frequently asked question is, "We're stuck. What should we do next?" In our roles as facilitators of communities of practice focused on instructional improvement, in our work on internal accountability (Richard) and using data (Liz), and in our research, we have noticed some distinct patterns in the way schools develop as they become more successful at improving student learning and measured performance. Here are a few of our observations.

There are no "breakthroughs" or dramatic "turnarounds" in the improvement of low-performing schools. There are, however, predictable periods of significant improvement, followed by periods of relative stasis or decline, followed again by periods of improvement. This pattern of "punctuated equilibrium" is common across all types of human development: individual, organizational, economic, and sociopolitical.

167

A very low-performing school may see significant improvements in students' scores in the early stages of concerted work to improve instruction. These early periods of growth are almost always the result of making more efficient use of *existing resources*—instructional time, teachers' knowledge and skill, and leadership focus. For example, a school might extend time spent on math from 45 minutes a day to 60 minutes, or might make smaller groups for literacy instruction. Not surprisingly, the improvements in performance that occur as a result of improvements in existing resources are relatively short term. They are usually followed by a period of flattened performance.

If a school is on a significant improvement trajectory, this plateau usually represents a process of incorporating new knowledge into the previous base of knowledge and skill. The school that extended time spent on math might now focus on what the math instruction looks like—how to teach mathematics so that students have a conceptual understanding of the math rather than only a procedural understanding. These changes are, by their very nature, extremely challenging. They challenge teachers' and administrators' existing ideas about what it is possible to do. They raise difficult questions about the effectiveness of past practices. They require unprecedented investments of time and energy. And often they do not produce immediate payoffs in measured student performance.

In our experience, most of the learning that schools do occurs during the periods of flat performance, *not* during periods when performance is visibly improving. Periods of visible improvements in performance usually occur as a consequence of earlier investments in knowledge and skill.

SURVIVING THE SLUMPS

Periods of flat performance in the improvement cycle raise some of the most difficult challenges educators face. It feels

WHAT SCHOOL IMPROVEMENT REALLY LOOKS LIKE

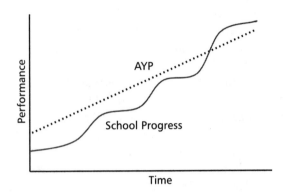

horrible when you and your colleagues are working harder than you have ever worked, when you have accepted the challenge of incorporating new practices into your work with students, when you are participating in planning and collegial activities that force you to move outside your comfort zone—and you see no visible payoff for these huge investments. These are the periods when it is important to develop a supportive work environment and positive leadership.

We've observed several practices in schools that thrive through stages of flat performance: (1) They expect the flat periods and persist through them; (2) they have a theory about how what they're doing will result in improved student performance; (3) they develop finer-grained measures for detecting improvement; and (4) they make adjustments when evidence suggests that their efforts really aren't working.

Expecting the flats and persisting. As schools gain experience with cycles of improvement and stasis (or decline), they recognize that the process of school improvement is the process of uncovering and solving progressively more difficult and challenging problems of student learning, which in turn demand new learning from adults. Once the initial gains have reached a plateau, teachers and administrators may begin to focus on a particular set of problems, often associated with broad categories of students, that require deliberate changes in practice.

For example, schools might determine that students are struggling with high-level thinking. One school might respond to this problem by focusing on the tasks teachers are asking students to do every day in the classroom: Are students being asked to do high-level thinking on a regular basis? What do high-level tasks look like in different subjects and grade levels? Another school might respond to the same problem by focusing on questioning: What kinds of questions are teachers asking in class? How might teachers incorporate more high-level questioning into their instruction? Another school might notice that teachers are framing high-level tasks and questions, but not checking to see whether students understand them. This school might focus on appropriate forms of in-class assessment. It takes time for these new practices to mature and become part of the working repertoire of teachers and administrators. Schools that are improving recognize and allow for this time and don't switch gears if they don't see immediate results on state tests.

Having a theory. It's a lot easier to stay the course if the course is something you anticipated. As educators gain experience, they are more able to explain how what they're doing will lead to the results they want and choose professional development approaches accordingly. We've seen this trajectory in schools' use of the professional development strategy of coaching. At first, schools and districts may adopt coaching because it's a popular strategy and they think that teachers need support around instruction, which coaches can provide. Coaching often doesn't provide the hoped-for outcomes, however, until the school can articulate a theory about *how* the coaching is supposed to help. For example, if the theory is that coaching helps by modeling good instruction and that teachers who see this instruction will adopt that practice, which will then lead to student learning—all that is examinable. Does the teacher's practice change after the modeling? Is there evidence of a difference in student learning? Having a theory also helps identify what improvements to look for in the gap between working hard and seeing state test results, so that you know whether to persist or change course. (For the record, our experience is that modeling alone rarely leads to change in instructional practice, but the point here is to have a theory that both shapes what form your action takes and is testable.)

Developing finer-grained measures for detecting improvement. In our experience, changes in student performance lag behind changes in the quality of instructional practice. Improvements are typically visible in classrooms before they show up on external measures. Improvement is not always as obvious as we would like, in part because we look in the wrong places (annual state tests rather than the daily work of teachers and students in classrooms); in part because we use tools that are designed to detect big changes, rather than the tiny ones that lead to the big ones (the equivalent of using a clock with no second hand to measure improvement in the speed at which you can run a mile); and in part because sometimes things get a little worse before they get better. We see this last pattern frequently when teachers go from asking students questions to which there is a correct answer to asking questions for which there are multiple possible answers. At first, teachers aren't very good at asking the questions or setting up a classroom environment in which ambiguity and intellectual risk-taking are valued, and students aren't very good at providing answers that require sentences rather than two-word responses, or at offering rationales for their answers.

Visible measures of progress are critical for motivating and encouraging educators to persist in the challenging work of improvement. Even the most dedicated and optimistic among us will stop if there's no sign that what we're doing is making a difference, or might make a difference eventually.

Making adjustments. In fact, schools that are improving do stop if there's no sign that what they're doing is making a difference. Having a theory and the right tools to test it makes it possible to identify the need for adjustments. Improving schools are willing to make adjustments, including stopping a course of action, if over time the evidence suggests their strategy isn't working.

THE NEXT LEVEL OF WORK

Sometimes, however, schools aren't sure what adjustments to make. What should schools do when they get stuck? "Stuckness" typically happens when people feel like they are doing their best work and it's not paying off in visible evidence of improved student performance. Billie Jean King—perennial tennis champion and accomplished coach—describes the transformation that occurred in her own career when she learned to regard errors as "feedback." This turned her frustration into reflection, and her reflection into increased focus and correction. Evidence that our best efforts are not producing what we want them to produce is feedback. The evidence is trying to tell us something about what we are doing, and if we listen to it, reflect on it, and give it voice, it will help us understand what to do next.

In our work, we help practitioners frame the next level of work by examining what they are currently doing, looking at evidence of student learning for clues about what is strongest in their practice and where they might see opportunities for improvement, strengthening the capacity of colleagues to work collectively on instructional issues, and increasing the specificity, or "grain size," of the instructional practices they are working on.

It is not unusual for schools to be doing very good work in a given content area—math or literacy—and for that work to be manifested in visible improvements in student performance. As time passes, however, teachers and administrators discover that what they considered to be their "best" work is not reaching certain students, or that performance overall is stuck in the middle range and not moving into the advanced range. These kinds of problems typically require closer examination of what students who are doing their "best" work are actually doing. What teachers typically discover is that the actual tasks that students are being asked to do, while considerably more challenging than those they were previously asked to do, are not at a level that will lead to the kind of student performance that teachers hope for. Or they find that the tasks are challenging, but the work is not scaffolded in a way that allows students to reach higher levels of performance. Or that students in some classrooms are able to do challenging tasks, but comparable students in other classrooms are not. The next level of work in each of these situations is different.

IMPROVEMENT AND ACCOUNTABILITY

As schools improve, three different but related processes are occurring. First, the level of knowledge and skill that teachers and administrators bring to the work of instructional practice is increasing. Second, teaching is moving from an individual to a collective activity, and internal accountability—the level of agreement and alignment across classrooms around powerful practices—is increasing. Finally, the school is aligning its organizational resources around support for instructional improvement.

All of these processes take time. And, as noted above, they do not occur in a straightforward, linear way. Just as with individual students, individual schools really do differ in the challenges they face and in their capacity to incorporate new practices.

Our accountability systems, as they are currently designed and implemented, do not reflect the real demands of school improvement. Well-designed accountability systems would start from an empirical knowledge of what school improvement looks like when it's happening and establish incentives and supports that accord with that knowledge. At the moment, the process is reversed: Accountability systems establish arbitrary timetables and impose powerful negative incentives on school improvement without any grounding in knowledge of how the process occurs. People in schools are forced to invent the knowledge themselves and must often work against the structures and incentives of the accountability system in order to get the job done.

The discipline of school improvement lies in developing strong internal processes for self-monitoring and reflection— *not* in meeting an artificially imposed schedule of improvement. That existing accountability systems don't reflect this reality is one of the great political tragedies of current education policy.

So, how long does it take? Educators know deep down that this is not the right question because it implies a finish line or a summit that we will someday reach. But that's not how improvement works. Some days we may feel like Sisyphus, forever pushing the boulder up the mountain, never to reach the top. But other days we get to what we thought was the summit and realize that still greater things are possible, things we couldn't see from below.

This is why we teach and lead. Improvement, after all, is essentially learning.

This chapter originally appeared in the May/June 2007 issue of the Harvard Education Letter.

FOR FURTHER INFORMATION

R.F. Elmore. *School Reform from the Inside Out: Policy, Practice, and Performance.* Cambridge, MA: Harvard Education Press, 2005.

P.B. Sebring, E. Allensworth, A.S. Bryk, J.Q. Easton, and S. Luppescu. *The Essential Supports for School Improvement.* Chicago: Consortium on Chicago School Research, 2006. Available online at http://ccsr.uchicago.edu/content/publications.php?pub_id=86

T. Wagner, R. Kegan, L.L. Lahey, and R.W. Lemons. *Change Leadership: A Practical Guide to Transforming Our Schools.* San Francisco: Jossey-Bass, 2006.

About the Authors

Mitch Bogen is an education writer based in Somerville, Mass.

Kathryn Parker Boudett is the director of the Data Wise Project at the Harvard Graduate School of Education, where she teaches educators how to use data. Boudett previously served as a consultant to the Boston Plan for Excellence.

Caroline Chauncey is the editor of the *Harvard Education Letter* and assistant director of the Harvard Education Publishing Group.

Elizabeth A. City is a doctoral student at the Harvard Graduate School of Education. A former teacher, principal, and coach, she currently teaches aspiring principals in Boston's School Leadership Institute.

Laura Cooper is the assistant superintendent at Evanston Township High School in Evanston, Ill.

Andreae Downs is a freelance writer living in Massachusetts. She is also a contributing writer to the *Boston Globe*.

Richard F. Elmore is the Gregory Anrig Professor of Educational Leadership at the Harvard Graduate School of Education and a senior research fellow at the Consortium for Policy Research in Education. His book *School Reform from the Inside Out* is published by Harvard Education Press.

Michael Fullan, professor emeritus of the Ontario Institute for Studies in Education of the University of Toronto, is currently special advisor to the premier and minister of education in Ontario, Canada. His book *Leading in a Culture of Change* was awarded the 2002 Book of the Year Award by the National Staff Development Council, and *Breakthrough* (with P. Hill and C. Crévola) won the 2006 Book of the Year Award from the American Association of Colleges for Teacher Education.

Richard J. Murnane, an economist, is the Thompson Professor of Education and Society at the Harvard Graduate School of Education. He is coauthor, with Frank Levy, of *Teaching the New Basic Skills* (Free Press), among other books.

Laura Pappano writes about education and is a coauthor, with Eileen McDonagh, of *Playing with the Boys: Separate Is Not Equal in Sports*, forthcoming from Oxford University Press.

Robert Rothman is a principal associate at the Annenberg Institute for School Reform at Brown University and the editor of *City Schools,* published by Harvard Education Press.

Michael Sadowski is an assistant professor in the Master of Arts in Teaching Program at Bard College in Annandale-on-Hudson, N.Y. He was formerly the editor of the *Harvard Education Letter*, an instructor on LGBT issues in schools at the Harvard Graduate School of Education, and vice chair of the Massachusetts Governor's Commission on Gay and Lesbian Youth.

Anand Vaishnav is currently the chief of staff to the superintendent of the Boston Public Schools. Before earning a master's degree in education policy and management at the Harvard Graduate School of Education, he was an education reporter for the *Boston Globe.*

Nancy Walser is the assistant editor of the *Harvard Education Letter*. She has served for eight years on the Cambridge (Mass.) School Committee and is vice president of the Massachusetts Association of School Committees.